AF256395

VIDMAKER 101

By
John Klawitter

VIDMAKER 101

ISBN: 978-0-9830372-6-2

Printed in the United States of America

Dancing Bear Publishing
A division of Dancing Bear Ent., LLC
Paw it right.

*For Lynn, who knows enough stories
to write a how-to book titled
The Vidmaker's Wife*

About The Author

A true "Hollywood Hyphenate", a Show Biz jack-of-all-trades, multi-talented John Klawitter migrated from the Midwest to Tinseltown where he applied his can-do spirit to write, produce and direct commercials, movie trailers, and television shows.

Today he works out of his hillside home studio, using his personal experiences to create award-winning books, novels, scripts and screenplays.

He is a member of the Director's Guild of America, the Writer's Guild of America, the Author's Guild, ASCAP, and the Epic Author's Combine. He is a contributing writer to the Twisted Tails Anthologies and his essays appear on rstturningpoint.com

Table of Contents

INTRODUCTION

This is an instruction manual for today's visual storyteller. I intend it to be a helpful instructional manual for the average person who enjoys lurking about with a video or stills camera…a person with hidden inner not-so-average ideas and a great deal of potential as a storyteller. This book is dedicated to the do-it-yourselfer and to the can-do spirit that resides in us all. It is meant to be a positive guide to show you—if you're interested in such things—how to shape and channel your creative impulses. Think of it as a cheerleading squad for the voices inside you that want to be heard, for your fresh new ideas that you hope will be seen and enjoyed by others.

Today's owners of still and video cameras have a huge untapped potential to tell visual stories in an exciting way. The problem is, few veteran video makers (In my part of the world we call them *vidmakers*) with actual experience are interested in showing others exactly how to do this. But the truth is, these skills are natural as telling a story. What's more, they are easy to understand and readily available to you. Deny it as they will, most vidmakers don't want to share their secrets because that would promote competition, and that makes them nervous. Worse, most high school and college film classes are led astray by the thrill of the shoot, by zoom lens envy and by the glittery fools gold of easy special effects.

It is true that there exists a gap between you—the enterprising guy or gal who owns video and stills cameras—and the so-called professionals who shoot visuals and weave them into stories for television. But it's *not that big* a gap. Even the hundreds of film festivals around the U.S. and the world are dominated by entries from what I call *bewildered sophisticates,* unfortunates often fueled by testosterone and ignorance to believe they are the next Stephen Spielberg. Nothing wrong with that, other than the fact that nobody's telling them how to get from where they are to where they want to be. Believe me—the gap between you and the pros is not nearly as great as they would have you believe, and you can make that leap.

Why not you? True, you're not in the Hollywood crowd, and you're not yet a *vid shooting wonder*. But you have good ideas, a dash of common sense, and an interest in people and the way things work. Why do your snapshots have to end up in a forgotten drawer? Why must your vidmaking be limited to cute family stills you email your relatives or an occasional shot of somebody getting whacked in the crotch that you send in to America's Funniest Home Videos?

Why waste a great video shot like the one above on a million-to-one-gamble sending it to America's Favorite Home Videos? With a little thought in the right direction, you can produce a wonderful little video about dad getting whacked in the balls with a little league baseball bat and how that made him a better person, or maybe the one you caught of your cousin swinging on a rope and crashing into a tree like George of the Jungle—and after that he spoke perfect Armenian and solved crossword puzzles. If you've captured some special moment on video, you already have the climactic, otherwise-impossible shot that will make your story work. Think about it—you have already captured a classic moment that is the heart of any story and will make your entry a film fest contestant and maybe even a big winner! And, even if you never shot your kid brother trying to ski off the roof, there are many other types of stories you can tell that you'll be able to give a special twist that is all your own.

Today you can take advantage of simple computer software editing systems that allow you to input dozens of family photos. Some programs are pre-set with fades and camera moves, somewhat like screensavers with automatic picture change, and they even give you the option of background theme music. Don't get me wrong; these are nice—more than nice, I see them as a step in the direction of good, solid storytelling, and if you haven't done so already, it's worth a little effort to put one together.

Take some time and upload some dozens of your camera stills, maybe family snaps at a picnic or gathered around a swimming pool in the back yard. Even in this automatic playback form, you are starting to tell a story. A few more steps in the right direction, and you will be telling how "Willie Wins the Blueberry Pie Eating Contest", or "Two Girls at the Carnival". Once you start telling visual stories this way with the camera and inexpensive software editing tools easily at hand, the only limits will be your interests and your imagination. Do you want to realistically document the things you see around you? Are you interested not so much in the way things are but in the way they should be? Is there a harsh or beautiful lesson in nature or in some selfless act of kindness that has moved you? All these directions will be available for you to tell your own stories.

You have the tools at hand to transform the tales already spinning around in your head into a reality. Today's vidmakers *get on out there* armed with home computers and mega pixel electronic stills cameras as well as video cameras with excellent zoom capability, automatic lighting and ultra-sharp lenses. You, yourself, have a good visual eye, probably better than you realize. Haven't you wanted to record what you see and the things you imagine and the even more fantastic visions you dream? Haven't you at some time or other mused how good it would feel to record and produce the stories you see around you in this exciting new form of electronic media. This is your age, my friend, your time to be a visual storyteller.

THIS COULD BE YOUR STORY. BUT INSTEAD OF A FEW NICE STILLS SHOTS, YOU COULD EASILY SHOOT ENOUGH STILLS AND VIDEO FOOTAGE TO PUT TOGETHER THE STORY OF HOW YOUR SON OR GRANDSON WON THE MEDAL AND HIS REWARD OF COOKIES AND JUICE. THAT MIGHT NOT SEEM LIKE MUCH FOR NOW, BUT WOULD CERTAINLY BE THUNDEROUSLY NICE FOR YOUR GREAT, GREAT, GREAT GRANDCHILDREN TO SEE WHAT LIFE HERE TODAY WAS LIKE.

Why not? I ask you. What's standing in your way? It doesn't matter how old you are—whether you just took your first video class or have been the family photographer for decades, recording every birthday and holiday as they came into focus.

Maybe you have the impulse, the talent and your own ideas about the world you see around you, and yet you feel dissatisfied; maybe you'd like to record the story of your town or a small video about the beauty in nature as you see it; maybe you'd like to tell a small parable about something important you learned in your own life, something you think of as vital to our own times that will be lost forever unless you pass it on…if you feel any of these things, you may gain value from the lessons in this small manual. And I am the right teacher for you; a natural do-it-myselfer blessed (or cursed) with never-say-die persistence, I've been there and done that, over and over again. *And you most certainly can, too!*

DO YOU REMEMBER HEARING ABOUT SOMETHING LIKE THIS? IT HAPPENED NEARLY 100 YEARS AGO, THE STORY YOUR GREAT GRANNY TOLD YOU OF HOW THAT DEAR MAN SHE CALLED HER "BOUNDER SCAMP" STOLE HER HEART AND HER PRICELESS PEARL NECKLACE, AND THEN, FELLED BY GUILT OR DESIRE, CAME CREEPING BACK TO BEG HER FORGIVENESS. WHAT WOULD IT TAKE TO CREATE A VIDEO THAT WOULD DO JUSTICE TO THAT AMAZING TALE OF PASSION AND TREACHERY—AND REDEEMING LOVE?

It's all storytelling, and if you've picked this book up, chances are at one time or another you've felt you could tell stories with the best of them. The problem is, the real ordinary life you and I live is a few steps away from *the storytelling mode.* That's one reason why the stories you see on television and in the movies, whether drama or comedy, are so—so *slick* it's like their storytelling is somehow different. It's like *those* storytellers must live in a different world. Actually not true, but it can give you a complex. A couple of things to make clear—this is a practical book, and I'm assuming you don't have a spare million bucks and six months of your life to spring your next story to life.

It can be disheartening to see the film festivals populated with hard-eyed, self-centered lunatics from some other universe. That's certainly not me, and not you, either. I just want to spin a visual tale or two. I think we might be able to do it as good as or even a bit better than the next person…the dreams we dream can't be so far off as they sometimes might seem.

THINK IN THE STORY TELLING MODE BEFORE YOU BEGIN: EVERYBODY KNEW THE GUY WAS A LETCH, BUT HE WASN'T EVERYBODY'S PROBLEM. IT WAS YOUR FIRST SUMMER JOB OUT OF HIGH SCHOOL, AND THAT DIRTY OLD MAN TOOK ADVANTAGE. JUST THINKING ABOUT IT TODAY, YEARS LATER, YOU STILL GET ANGRY. YOU KNOW YOU COULD TELL THIS STORY.

Let's not forget one thing here: You do have your own unique take on things, your own vision and talent. Believe me, I know you can bring your ideas to reality. You can make bright, professional visual storytelling a part of your life. You can be a vidmaker.

Now I'm not saying it's easy. The process of creating really good visual stories involves more than just one or two mumbling rituals. The steps are all important, even should you use the lessons in this book to become a *filmic legend* like Ronnie Howard or Sandra Bullock. And they're not infallible, either. When *celebs* like that screw up and miss a step or two, that's when they come up with rotten tomatoes. If you take the steps one by one, you can and will tell your visual stories in an interesting way that will impress and entertain your viewers. You'll be able to post on sites like YouTube and Vimeo, to enter Film Festivals—and who knows what may lie beyond?

WHY COULDN'T YOU DO A SOFT AND GAUZY TONE POEM OF THE JOYFUL DAYS OF YOUR OWN YOUTH? STORY TELLING IS LIKE THAT; YOU CAN LOOK BACK THROUGH THE PRISM OF YOUR EXPERIENCE AND HAVE LEARNED SOMETHING FROM YOUR LIFE THAT YOU CAN PASS ON.

This book isn't about video gear or computer software. It is about the process—the mindset and the steps that it takes to become a successful visual storyteller. If you want to be that person, this is the little lesson book that will show you the way. The journey will provide you with a new way to share your most important ideas with people everywhere who have live minds and imaginations, viewers with active ideas who care to see what your own personal take on life is all about.

THERE WILL ALWAYS BE NEWER, BETTER EQUIPMENT. BUT GOOD STORYTELLING HASN'T CHANGED SINCE PEOPLE FIRST HUDDLED ABOUT CAMPFIRES TO HEAR OF MONSTERS AND STRANGE DRAGONS.

Vidmaker 101 is an instruction manual that uses examples to illuminate and illustrate along the way. Vidmaking can be hard work, but it is also fun and enjoyable, and so I'll share some creative experiences that you may find humorous, outrageous or just downright dumb. You'll see that, while I've written, produced and directed an interesting bunch of work, I've tripped up pretty badly here and there along the way.

For the serious and the ambitious, Vidmaker 101 provides a chapter relating to each step in the visual storytelling process, arranged for the most part in chronological order. And there is a proposed assignment at the end of each chapter. Read for your own personal amusement, if you will. But those who accept and complete the assignments will, by the end of this instructional book, have completed the first of their own visual stories, whether a brief documentary, a short visual tone poem or a dramatic short video.

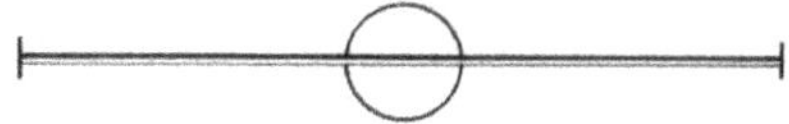

1 - START HERE

> **"There is less real difference between the famous expert and an ordinary person than the so-called *experts* would have you believe."**
>
> *--Richard (Dick) Feynman, Theoretical Physicist, Cosmic Philosopher and highly regarded bongo drummer.*

With today's video equipment, just about anybody can make a short film. Look at all the *one-time-wonders* who borrow Uncle Wilber's video camera and end up on YouTube. But this is not about lucky snappers or easy short cuts. This is a book for serious-minded storytellers, for creative people who want to think through their own good ideas and then shepherd them faithfully to finished videos, rather than having the process run away with them. I promise that if you soak in these ideas like a sponge you'll empower yourself to create wonderful vids every time. Remember, good stories don't just *happen.*

DON'T BUILD YOUR REPUTATION ON UNRELIABILITY. THE HOLGA IS A CHEAP CHINESE CAMERA FAMOUS FOR TAKING ODDLY UNPREDICTABLE SHOTS FULL OF STREAKS AND IMAGES SO WEIRD THAT SOME ARE CONVINCED IT IS HAUNTED BY GHOSTS. YOU DON'T WANT TO "HOLGA" YOUR WAY TO VIDMAKING. BE SHARP, STAY IN FOCUS, AND YOU CAN BREAK THE RULES LATER.

Either you are in charge or you will end up with a video that's not much like your original idea, assuming you had something in mind in the first place that was a bit more solid than the vague idea *I want to make a video.* You may be startled to find out that, while the tools to shoot and edit may be constantly changing, there is no substitute for a good story, well thought out, well written and well directed.

YOU DON'T HAVE TO BE AN OLD FUD, A DERLICT-OF-ANOTHER-TIMES OR A POET LIKE HENRY WADSWORTH LONGFELLOW TO ORGANIZE YOUR THINKING BEFORE YOU BEGIN YOUR PROJECT. BY THE WAY, HAVE YOU EVER READ HENRY OUT LOUD WHILE WALKING THE DOG OR WAITING FOR THE DOWNLOAD TO HAPPEN? NOT HALF BAD, OLD WADSWORTH.

Letting the process control you could be okay, if you can be happy dreaming of a Ferrari and ending up with a dented old Honda Civic. Not that you can't have a good story and make it better along the way…but if you don't have a clear idea and a firm hand on the production process, your adaptation will end up different and worse rather than improved and better. Writers and filmmakers alike who let their story run out of control are sometimes called *pantsers*, because they fly by the seat of their pants, and if you are totally 100% one of those, this isn't the instruction manual for you.

<u>**THINK ABOUT THIS**</u>: **WHEN TALENTED SCULPTOR HOBART BROWN INVENTED HIS CLASSIC KINETIC SCULPTURE RACE, *WAS HE A BRILLIANT CREATIVE OR DID HE ALLOW HIS GENIUS TO RUN WILD?* YOU DO WELL TO KNOW YOURSELF, TO REALIZE WHAT TYPE OF CREATIVE PERSON YOU MOST LIKELY ARE AND WOULD LIKE TO BE. YOUTUBE IS CROWDED WITH ONE-SHOT WONDERS; HOLLYWOOD, LESS SO, AND YET THE *WILD CHILD PHENOMENA* EXISTS. WHATEVER PROCESS YOU CHOOSE, IF YOU WANT TO BE AROUND A WHILE, TRY TO REMEMBER WHAT YOU DID THAT WORKED FOR YOU. AND DON'T LET YOUR EGO RULE YOU. THAT MEANS *START OVER BY GOING BACK TO STEP ONE EVERY TIME YOU START A NEW PROJECT.***

Your idea, also known as your 'concept', is more important than any other consideration. While it is true that certain short films are more open to wild creativity and snooping around with a camera than others, it is also true that, before you start, it's best to have a clear idea what you want to create. You know the old Zen wisdom, *If you don't know where you're going, you'll never get there.*

If you decide your venture is all about making money, that's fundamentally okay. After all, if you keep blowing your paycheck or your inheritance on vids that drain your pockets, chances are you won't be able to continue after the first bunch of projects. But making money isn't a *creative concept,* it's a pragmatic objective.

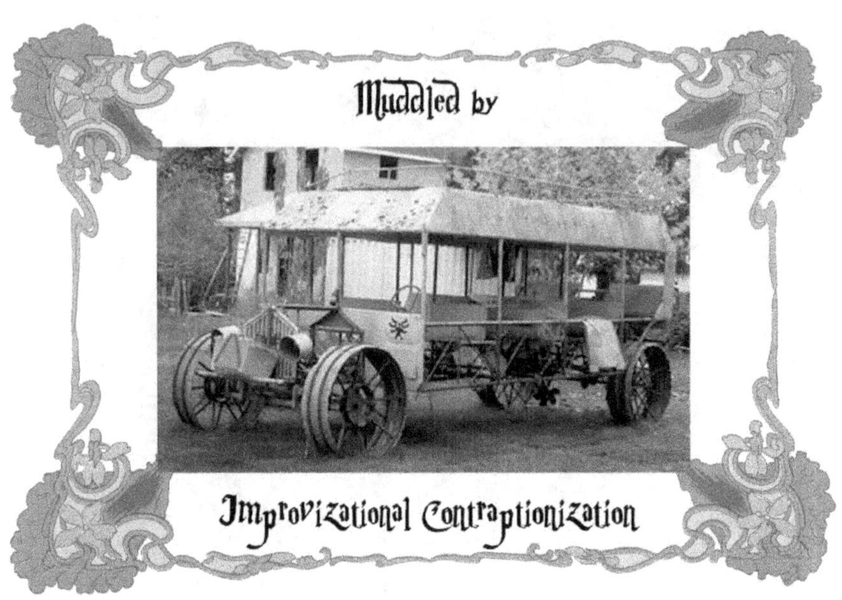

<u>KNOW WHAT YOU WANT TO DO, AND DO IT—NO MATTER WHAT!</u> IF YOUR VISION IS TO CREATE A FLOWER POWER RACER THAT CAN BE PEDALLED ALONG BY THE HAPPY CITIZENS OF UTOPIA, THAT'S OKAY. BUT IF THE OBJECTIVE IS TO CREATE A VID WITH TRANSFORMERS AND YOU END UP WITH VEHICLES OUT OF CHITTY CHITTY BANG BANG, THAT'S NOT A GOOD THING, PARTICULARLY IF YOU HOPE TO BE TAKEN SERIOUSLY BY YOUR VIEWERS. WAS THIS HOBART BROWN'S ORGINAL INTENTION, OR DID HE MAKE IT UP AS HE WAS GOING ALONG? THE QUESTION MAY NOT HAVE BEEN AS IMPORTANT TO HOBART, LIVING IN SOMEWHAT RELAXED EARLIER TIMES, AS IT COULD BE TO YOU AS YOU STRUGGLE TO MAKE SUPERIOR VIDS IN TODAY'S CREATIVE WILDERNESS.

Let's say you start out to do a documentary, an exposé about the plight of women in some remote country in Africa. You quietly slip away from your safari tour and set out with your camera on the ready, intent upon shooting documentary style. But the sad condition of these impoverished black women proves too depressing, so you end up unearthing and filming a wrinkled old storyteller who narrates some wonderfully fresh tribal myths that you later illustrate by translating quaint native drawings to film. There's nothing morally wrong with your path, unless you're being funded by a woman 's rights organization expecting to see a dramatic portrayal of the harsh lives of certain African women. However, it's clearly not what you set out to do.

This brief guide is intended to be a shining light in the dark forest of distractions, the swamp of denial and the seemingly impossible obstacles real life will throw in the way of your artistic adventures. From time to time I've been a raving lunatic *pantser* myself, and some good must have come of it or I wouldn't be able to write this book. But my shelves and files are littered with half finished projects that were started out of blind enthusiasm, and I have dozens of films, documentaries and even TV Specials that, with advanced planning and a bit more organization, might have seen a better success.

<u>**HOW WELL DO YOU KNOW YOUR CREATIVE SELF?**</u> **ARE YOU DOMINATED BY YOUR CLASSIC CREATIVE MODE? ARE YOU A 100% PANTSER? OR JUST WHERE ARE YOU IN BETWEEN? DOUBTFUL AS IT SEEMS, I AM ACTUALLY 75% CLASSIC, AND ONLY ONE FOURTH PANTSER. NO, REALLY.**

In a way, it is easier to write a documentary than a dramatic film. This is because the story you wish to 'document' is already out there. It already exists, and it's your job to find, film and present it to your audience. Of course, I'm talking about pure documentaries like Ken Burns work on the history of baseball or the Civil War. If you are into propaganda documentary filmmaking like Michael Moore, your narrative and your footage selection can be more difficult, as your purpose is to persuade as well as educate.

Adapting a short story to a short dramatic film format can be difficult. The finished film will not faithfully represent the original unless you have clarity at the beginning. That is why makers of short films and videos will sometimes start by writing their own original script as a short story. Unfortunately, creatives may have *an idea for a film, but no clear idea how it turns out.* This leads to the suggestion you might begin your film or vid project with a short summary of the story itself.

I like to start my vids with an idea that becomes a story outline that becomes a short story (or a novel). However, even if you develop your idea this way, not all of your ideas will be candidates you'll be able to turn into video shorts.

<u>**NOT EVERY ONE OF YOUR IDEAS CAN BECOME A VID**</u>**: WHEN I WON RECOGNITION FOR ONE OF MY SHORT STORIES FROM THE PRESTIGIOUS HEMINGWAY SHORT STORY CONTEST, I HAD HIGH HOPES THAT I MIGHT CONVERT IT INTO A BRILLIANT SHORT VIDEO. BUT THIS DID NOT HAPPEN.**

I have written certain short stories that I favor, that I believe are as true to the mark as any short story ever written. I wrote one called "Jack's Boat", a story about my love-hate relationship with my father. It won a mention at the Hemingway Short Story Contest—the real one they hold down in the Florida Keys, not the one in which up and coming writers try to parody Hemingway's style. You have to wonder why I could not make this short story into a dramatic video.

I very much did want to adapt my short story into a video, but I wasn't interested in doing a jump-off idea, say a bemused short film about my Catholic father's friendship with the communist who lived across the back alley from us, or a little drama about the time we found out Dad was dying of a brain tumor. Those other ideas might make good or even great short films, but I would only be making them because I decided it was impossible to make "Jack's Boat".

TAKE A CLOSER LOOK AT THIS PHOTOGRAPH: THE STORY IS ABOUT A LIKEABLE YOUNG BALLPLAYER ON THE WAY UP UNTIL HE LOSES THREE FINGERS ON HIS PITCHING HAND IN AN ACCIDENT AT THE FLINTCOTE STAMPING PLANT. GOOD IDEA FOR A FILM, FOR SURE…BUT HOW MANY THINGS DO YOU SEE IN THE PHOTO ABOVE THAT YOU AS A LOW BUDGET NOVICE VIDMAKER MIGHT FIND HARD TO RENT OR REPLICATE?

You begin to see the reasons not make "Jack's Boat". *Budget, certainly.* After all, I'm not made of money, and maybe you're not, either. *And actors, certainly.* You couldn't just get any *schlump* to play the complex character that was my father. Then too, "Jack's Boat" has so many flashbacks that it might work better as a feature length movie. This is the kind of thinking you get into when, as a writer, you begin to mull adapting one of your own ideas into a video. Arguably, it's easier when some big-bucks producer says to you, *I love this story; here's a chunk of money, bring me a 1st draft in six weeks.* But that's not something you can count on.

There are a wild variety of important matters to consider before you plunge into turning your own idea into a short film. It isn't that the process itself is beyond anyone who is creative. Having written a good outline or short story, you should have the ability to get on with a visual version. But be alert; there are practical considerations that could intervene…things like money and your day job.

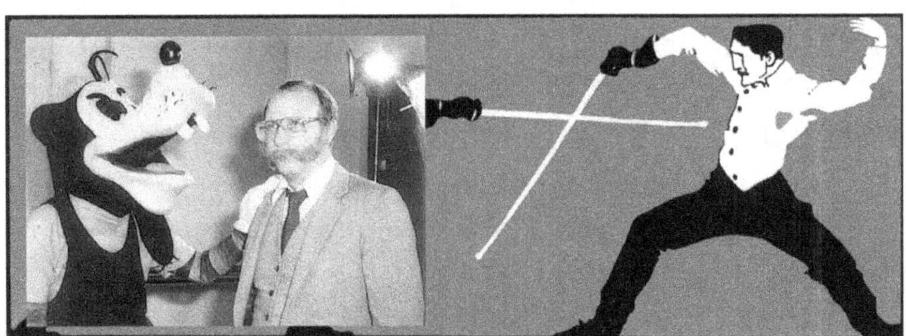

IT HAS TO BE SOMETHING YOU CAN ACTUALLY PRODUCE. IMAGINE YOU WROTE ABOUT GOOFY. WHO BETTER THAN YOU TO ADAPT IT INTO A SHORT VIDEO? SUPPOSE YOU VISUALIZED GOOFY AS AN OLYMPIC FENCER. CREATING A SHORT VID FROM THAT STORY MIGHT BE TOUGH. *HOW MUCH EASIER THEN*, TO HAVE A STORY ABOUT TWO FRIENDS ON A TRIP TO VEGAS AND ABOUT TO MEET A LIFE CHANGING EXPERIENCE! COULD YOU TELL THAT STORY ON A LIMITED BUDGET? CHANCES ARE, *YES YOU COULD.* AND YOU WOULDN'T NEED GOOFY, WHO MIGHT WANT HIS OWN STAR CABANA AND OTHER COSTLY PERKS.

On the plus side, once you have a solid outline, much of the concept and creative work, at least as it relates to the story, is well begun. You have your story arc, your conclusion, your O'Henry-ish snapper or Flannery O'Connor type life lesson

learned. But the art of vidmaking is often one of *interpretation* .
And it is up to you to decide *if* and *how far* you wish to stray
from your original vision. *What?!* I can almost hear you roar. *I
won't change a comma or a period!* Maybe that attitude is
stretching a little bit; still, if the creative inclinations in you wish
to remain as true as possible to your original idea, then you may
learn a few life-lessons from this slim volume.

      Pick the right story to tell, and with a little tenacity
you can create an interesting, professionally produced and even
award winning short film from one of your ideas. Chances are,
you're already something of a story teller, and you already know
what you want to say. Now you have to show courage and
conviction to follow through and bring that idea to life. But a
little caution at the outset: Do not underestimate the input of
bosses and friends; brainstorming can be helpful, but even the
most well-intentioned suggestions can cause you to drift from
your original idea.

All really good vidmaking is storytelling. When I started out to tell stories some forty years ago, I was too massively stubborn to let anybody convince me anything was impossible. I lucked into a cub copywriter job at one of the top ad agencies in the country, and from the beginning I believed you had to snag people with a good opening line, tell an interesting story, and finish with a flourish. And my stubborn determination proved to be a good thing, after all.

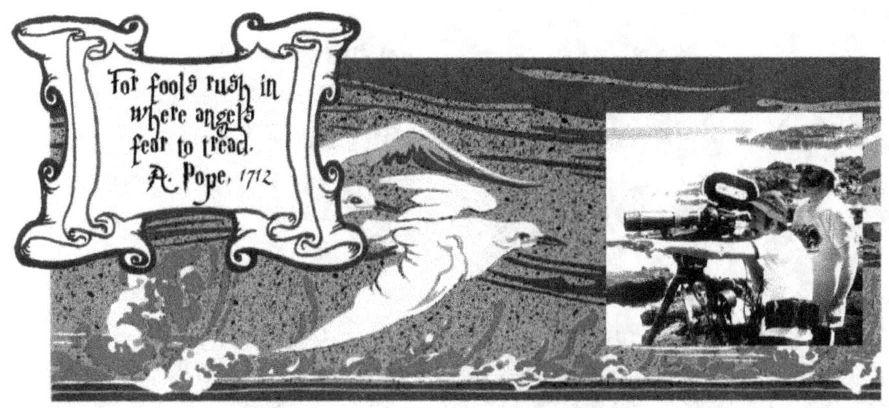

<u>**VIDMAKING CAN BE DANGEROUS.**</u> **I ONCE CREATED A TELEVISION AD CAMPAIGN THAT PROMISED THE TASTE OF A WINE WAS LIKE 'A GIANT WAVE OF REFRESHMENT' HERE I AM STANDING HEROICALLY BEHIND MY CAMERAMAN, WHO IS POINTING OUT TO SEA TO CONVINCE ME WE SHOULD SHOOT FROM SHORE BECAUSE IT IS TOO DANGEROUS TO GO OUT THERE WITH CAMERAS MOUNTED ON SURF BOARDS. HE WAS RIGHT AND I NEARLY DROWNED. AND YET, ALL THAT SAID, ONCE YOU COMMIT TO AN IDEA, YOU ARE RESPONSIBLE FOR FORMING IT INTO A VIDEO. YES, IT MAY BE HARD OR EVEN DANGEROUS. DON'T BE FOOLISH, BUT DON'T LET THAT STOP YOU, EITHER.**

Ideas, even good ones, are a dime a dozen. The skill and the hard work viewers never see involves working them up into stories that can then be developed into interesting videos. It's not an automatic thing; it's a process with a lot of small but vital steps, not entirely unlike an automobile assembly line.

When you start to tell your stories, you may find your friends and family are willing to help. This is great, but don't let the tidal wave of top-of-the-head ideas from others overwhelm you. Ideas are everywhere, and it is your job to create the unique world of your own video from your own original idea. The point of this is to encourage you to follow your instincts. You might have a silly or totally stupid idea (probably not), but chances are you have a good concept. Either way, figure that out for yourself. After all is said and done, it's you who must go through the effort and the agony of developing your idea into a completed video. *So shouldn't it be your ideas that count the most?!*

<u>**REMEMBER, IT IS YOUR STORY, NOT AUNT DORA'S.**</u> **YOU MAY BE A BIT INACCURATE REGARDING CERTAIN FACTS OF WHAT DID OR DID NOT HAPPEN AND MAYBE YOUR INTERPRETATION OF EVENTS IS DIFFERENT FROM WHAT THIS OR THAT PERSON WILL INSIST. POLITELY TAKE ALL INPUT UNDER CONSIDERATION, BUT STAY TRUE TO YOUR OWN STORY SENSE AND YOUR OWN INTERPRETATION. VIDMAKING DOES NOT WORK WELL WHEN MANY HEADS BELIEVE THEY ARE IN CHARGE.**

Your video is your interpretation of what happened, or of what you think may have happened, or of what you would have liked to have happened. This is what it means to *stay true to your tale*, to the spinning of events as you see them. How often have you watched a movie or a play and half way in you begin to feel there were too many cooks in the kitchen? When starting out, a wealth of notions and interpretations can be helpful; but when parallel ideas begin to conflict you know you're story is on its way to *muddleville*. This is why, as the master or mistress of your tale, you have to stay open to suggestions and yet isolate yourself from ideas you know are counter to the way you see it.

It is easy to be persuaded from your ideas when you first have them. After all, you are envisioning a world of your own imagination that only you can see. What do you think the people around you would say if you told them you wanted to do a short video about children's toys, or one that demonstrated how far suns and galaxies were separated from each other in outer space? It doesn't matter who you are or how you make your living, if you think you have a good video idea, the only way to really find out is to produce your visual story and make your idea a reality.

Wonderful great ideas for vids don't have to be heavy with literary intentions. In the 1930's, Charles Eames, inventor of classic chairs that bear his name, was a struggling young architect and furniture designer. When I began meeting with him at his studio in the 1970's, he showed me his award winning films, "Toy Trains" and "Powers of Ten". The first film transports you into the magic world of toy trains. And the second takes you on a wondrous trip across the universe. If you're thinking stuff like *Oh well, yeah, but that was the great Charles Eames,* you might want to consider that when he did those shorts he was just a guy making experimental chairs out of plywood and cardboard, hardly a wizard like Demille or Hitchcock.

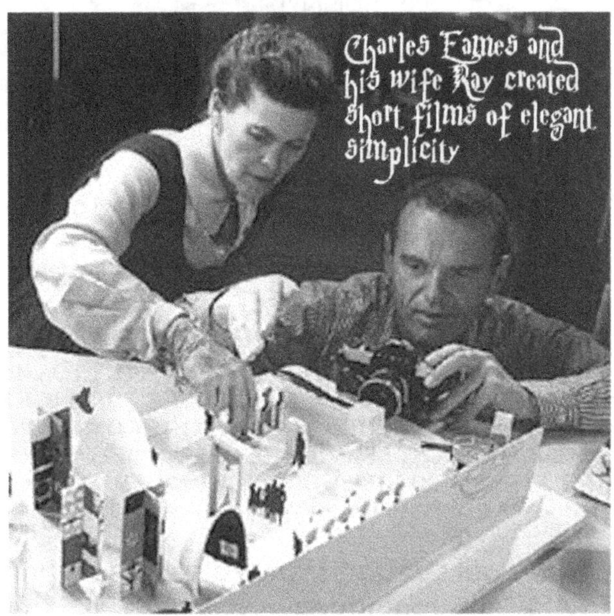

Should your critics prove troublesome, you have to find a solution to the problem of them. It doesn't matter if you're a furniture designer or a court reporter, if you think you have a good video idea, the only way to really find out is to produce your videos and make your ideas spring to visual life.

You're already a thinking person or you wouldn't have bought this book. And now that you have it, I'm here to walk you through the process of turning your ideas story into visual genius, or at least to show how I did it on any number of occasions. So toughen up by reading the *Seven Expert Reasons Why You Can't Do Whatever:*

SEVEN REASONS WHY YOU CAN'T DO IT

You don't have a degree. *Having graduated from college is a weapon used by those who have been there, especially now that there are degrees in things like Mouse Husbandry and Socializing On The Internet.*

You've obviously never done this before. *This is called "jinxing the first timer." Don't let it get you down.*

You don't have any credits on IMDB. *The insider's truth about IMDB is that it never tells how you got them.*

You've never been on the NY Times best seller list. *Neither was Edgar Allen Poe, James Fenimore Cooper or Henry James, so don't let that bother you.*

You look funny. *Older people should not use this one, now that it is so easy to look up pictures on the internet.*

You don't dress like us. *People who have time to dress fashionably probably can't teach you how to rack focus.*

You must have got that idea from somebody else. *Sure, like they're going to when they steal it from you..*

In the early 1970's, the process of *serious* visual storytelling was more difficult than it is today. You had to buy, rent or borrow a Bolex or Boleau 16 mm camera. You mostly had to spring-wind it yourself, so the takes were necessarily short. Film was expensive. You had to find a very dark place or use a film bag and load the film in the magazine yourself. Processing and editing were very expensive. The path from raw film to finished answer print was labor intensive and took weeks or even months, and involved a clunky machine called a moviola that physically ran edited work-print footage backwards and forwards in sync with a mag sound track. Not today. So you can concentrate less on mechanics and more on story.

Lucky you. Today you can pick up a wonderful high resolution video camera and inexpensive editing software to create your own masterpiece in a fraction of the time it took me to make my first films. And now I'll show you how to do it.

<u>I WORKED IN ADVERTISING</u>, AND CLIENTS PAID FOR WHAT I THINK OF AS MY BASIC VID TRAINING. HERE WE ARE SHOOTING A WINE COMMERCIAL FOR A NORTHERN CALIFORNIA VINTNER. FROM LEFT TO RIGHT, THE ART DIRECTOR WITH THE BIG STORYBOARDS, ME DIRECTING, THE CAMERAMAN WITH HIS HAND ON HIS CHIN AND THE JUNIOR ACCOUNT EXEC WONDERING IF I REALLY KNOW WHAT I'M TALKING ABOUT.

Being 'creative' will involve much more than adapting your short story; it also will apply to how you find the time and the funding to make your film happen, and to how you gain the experience to become an accomplished vidmaker.

There are people with a little extra money who want to be in *show business.* They will never in their lives have another chance like the one you present them, to be a part of your production and even becoming a *producer* by actually funding it.. And there are actors and actresses and crew members who will work for little or no money, if you ask them the right way. You may not want to convince your wealthy aunt to mortgage her cottage in Maine (she could cut you out of her will), but there are plenty of people you don't love so much who are itching to climb on board your exciting venture. I would encourage you to be relatively open and honest in appealing for help, but at the same time, don't hide the excitement and the thrill of working on an actual film from those who are tempted to assist you.

SEVEN DISCUSSIONS TO AVOID:

Maybe you should just start over.
I don't get what you're trying to do.
Right minded people don't think like you.
Here, I can show you how to fix it.
Nobody likes it when you do it that way.
You have to take other things into account.
No, Shakespeare thought of that before you.

Write down what type of short video you might like to make-and jot down some possible themes or subjects, things like "Animals of the Prairie Midlands", or "Demented People Who Shaped Me", or "Duck Hunting in Cairo"*

*If you think this is simply amusing, you should know that "Duck Hunting in Cairo" was the title of one of World famous artist-reporter Franklin McMahon, Sr.'s first audio-visual stories.

TWO – THE FORMULA

"It's simple—all filmmaking is made up of three elements: Time, Money, and Talent. In film and video production, the less of any of the three you have, the more you have to make up for it with the others."

--Nelson B. Winkless,jr, Creative Director at Leo Burnett and jingle writer of "Snap, Crackle, Pop—Rice Krispies!"

<u>WINK ADVISED THE YOUNG NOVICE CREATIVE ME</u> "DON'T EVER TRY TO TELL ANYBODY HOW TO CREATE ANYTHING UNLESS YOU'VE FIRST DONE IT YOURSELF." I FOUND THAT ATTITUDE WONDERFUL—HE ASSUMED I *WOULD AND COULD GO AFTER THE BRASS RING* AND LEARN EVERYTHING ABOUT CREATING VISUAL STORIES.

So about now you're saying to yourself, *Well, crap, it can't be that easy as Wink says.* Truth is, the entire process is fairly simple; but Nelson B. Winkless, jr. and I never implied it was *easy.* If it was simple as hearing and admiring *Snap, Crackle, Pop* or the *Bugs Bunny / Road Runner Show* opening song, you wouldn't need this book.

You do have to be *practical*. When you're writing a short story, the world is entirely at your disposal. If you want a spaceship like the one that crash lands on a distant planet in my book of parables, THE ROGUE PIRATES BIBLE HERETICAL, it's a matter of a few key strokes. But that could be one hell of an expensive shot for your video.

IT ONLY TAKES A FEW KEYSTROKES TO WRITE A SPACE CRAFT INTO A SHORT STORY OR TWO (LIKE I DID), BUT IF YOU WANT TO PUT A BELIEVABLE ONE IN YOUR VID, IT COULD COST YOU LOTS OF TIME AND MONEY. [SEE MY BOOK TRAILER ON YOUTUBE TO LEARN HOW I SOLVED THIS PROBLEM. http://www.youtube.com/watch?v=fFtngfuPKXc]

IF YOU CAN FIND A WAY TO FIT A SPOOFY STYLE OR A RETRO LOOK IN YOUR VID, YOU CAN CREATE MAGIC WITH LITTLE MONEY. IMAGINE THIS TOY SPACECRAFT BOBBING OVER A PAPER MACHETTE WORLD, SPARKS SPITTING AS IT SAGS TO A BOUNCY CRASH LANDING. WELL, YOU DON'T HAVE TO IMAGINE—THE OLD EPISODES OF BUCK ROGERS STILL EXIST. BUT WILL SUCH A STYLE WORK IN *YOUR STORY?*

When deciding which story idea you want to adapt to video, be aware of _The Three Elements_. The training I received from my years in advertising made me hyper-aware of these three filmmaking factors: _Time. Money. Talent._

THE THREE MIGHTY ELEMENTS OF FILM & VIDEO

TIME – _Time marches mercilessly against you._
MONEY – _Ideas are conceived in Creative Heaven. Budgets are forged in the lowest rungs of Financial Hell._
TALENT –_If it's your film, you're the primary talent. This is Your blessing and your curse. Always follow your own creative instincts._

In filmmaking, nobody ever has enough money. No matter whether you are doing a vid exposing your corrupt town mayor or adapting a Scott Turow novel to the big screen, your world will be filled with choices. You might want the hot girl down the block to play your vampire seductress, but do you have a back-up plan when you offer tickets to watch the Modesto Nuts baseball game but she wants a thousand dollar buying spree at the fanciest fine apparel shop in town? Remember, *It's your idea, your story—and your money.* Be aware of your budget from the first keystroke.

EVERY FILMMAKER STRUGGLES TO FIND THE RIGHT TALENT. DISNEY PRODUCER JAN WILLIAMS WANTED "A" ACTORS RAQUEL WELCH AND AND HARRISON FORD FOR HIS JAMES BOND SPOOF. WHEN ALL THE "A" ACTORS HE THOUGHT COULD FIT THE PART TURNED DOWN HIS OFFERS, HE WENT DOWN TO THE "B" LIST FOR MICHAEL CRAWFORD AND BARBARA CARRERA. AS A NEWLY MINTED VIDMAKER, YOU'LL FIND YOURSELF WITH SIMILAR SITUATIONS AND CONCERNS.

Time is never on your side. Sometimes it gets down to days, hours or minutes. If you schedule a three day shoot to take place in two days, the quality of your production is bound to suffer…unless you squeeze your talent and maybe get lucky with the weather and with that iguana that never seems to want to eat flies when your camera is rolling.

Backwards thinking can save your project. If you visualize the finished product and work backwards from there, you can save yourself a lot of trouble and even avoid a costly crash-and-burn. Let's say you have a dozen ideas that would make fantastic short dramatic films. How can you pick the one that will work best as a video? See the finished product in your mind and then figure out how to get there.

THINK OF THE VARIOUS DEPICTIONS THE GREATEST ARTISTS OF ALL TIME HAVE RENDERED TO ILLUSTRATE THE CREATION OF MANKIND AS ALMIGHTY GOD PRODUCED HIS MOST MAJESTIC CREATURES IN HIS OWN IMAGE IN JUST SIX DAYS AND SIX NIGHTS.

Why should Almighty God have all the fun? Perhaps it is the devil in me tempting you to find something godlike in the act of creating your own film or video. It is a world unto its own, is it not? It breathes, it lives, and with the last flickering frame, it dies. Your story has a beginning, a middle and an end. You can, perhaps feel the addictive tug beginning, what it means to be this sort of creative person. Don't miss the point: there's something wonderful about the act of creating your own story on your own film or video. Everything else is just brushstrokes, word structure, camera angles…you know, details.

IT IS NOT A SIN TO SEE YOURSELF AS THE CREATOR OF THE WORLD OF YOUR FILM OR VIDEO. HOWEVER, YOU MAY NOT BE ABLE TO AFFORD ALL SIX DAYS AND SIX NIGHTS ON YOUR LIMITED BUDGET.

The immutable laws of Time, Money & Talent are the fundamental dynamics of the production universe, and like gravity, magnetic and electromagnetic forces and quarkian mechanics, they will move inexorably to fulfill your destiny or crush you like an ant. So prepare yourself. You may be the supreme creative force behind your visual story, but even you must play by the rules.

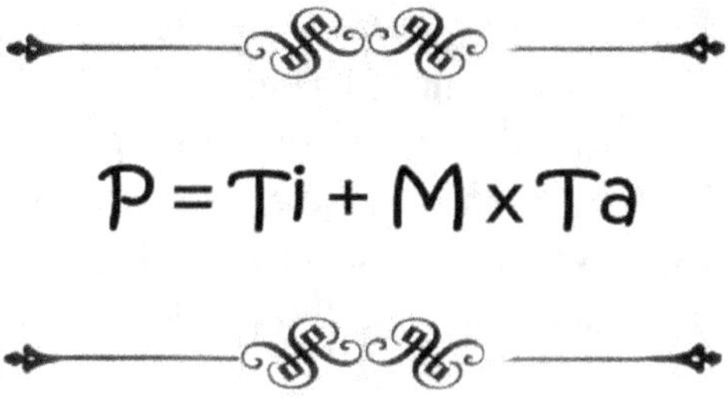

$$P = Ti + M \times Ta$$

IT IS TIME *PLUS* MONEY, BUT YOU HAVE TO MULTIPLY TALENT. BECAUSE THE LESS OF EITHER OF THE FIRST TWO, THE MORE YOU MUST MAKE UP WITH YOUR OWN ABILITY.

Construct a one-page chart of your week.
Write the numbers 1 through 24 vertically on the
left hand side of the page. Add seven more
vertical columns, one for each day of the week.
Across the top of the page write the various
obligations and habits that make up each day---
sleeping, eating, travel to and from work or
school, recreation. Use pastel colors to indicate
more clearly the various blocks of time spent.
This will give you an idea what sort of choices
you will make to create your first video story.

Evaluate your gear and equipment. You will need
a decent computer, a decent video camera, perhaps
a decent stills camera, and some editing software.

Don't worry at all about your talent. At this
point it's all about your will. If your story
needs telling badly enough, with your help it
will form out of the ether before your very eyes.

3 - THE IDEA BEHIND THE VID

"Yes, but are you *happy?*"
--Weary and seasoned filmmaker Larry Sands upon listening to the young me lecture on how to attack, conquer and get ahead in Hollywood.

What kind of visual stories do you want to tell?
When you are your own filmmaker, you have more possibilities than even the most prolific professionals who are tied to what they think will sell, to their careers, and to what viewers expect of them. You, on the other hand can do whatever your imagination and your mind tells you is interesting, exciting and worth doing. There is a great divide between documentaries and dramatic vids, but that's not the only choice to be made. Many vidmakers today take inspiration from pop, rock, hip-hop or classical music and cut their visuals to the beat, or dissolve between beautiful images from nature, animals or the human form. Some of the experimentally inclined are finding new forms of expression in basic shapes and forms, in new types of animation, and in mind-jarring and shocking visual expressionism. It's worth thinking about before you start.

I DIDN'T REALIZE I WAS TELLING STORIES WHEN I FIRST WORKED IN TELEVISION ADVERTISING, BUT THAT'S EXACTLY WHAT IT WAS. THE FORMULA MY AD AGENCY LOVED WAS A SNAPPY OPENING, SELLING POINTS IN THE MIDDLE AND A ZINGER BUTTON-OFF ENDING.

As a do-it-yourself vidmaker, you get to think up your own ideas and then actually create them. It may come as a surprise, but that is not the way 99% of all the visual stories you see on television or in the movie houses are made. While webvid is a little more freewheeling because there's less money for production, it is still an unfortunate reality that many vidmakers spend all their time bringing other people's ideas to life. There's nothing wrong with this, if you choose that direction; it's simply the way of the world. *Just remember, that doesn't have to be your way!*

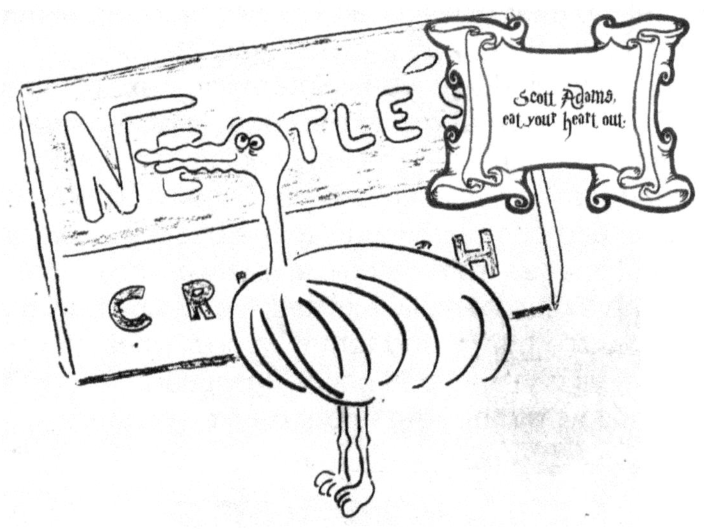

IN MY FIRST JOB AS CUB COPYWRITER, I PRESENTED MY AD CONCEPTS ALONG WITH HAND DRAWN SKETCHES THAT WERE QUESTIONABLY ON A PAR WITH JAMES THURBER OR SCOTT ADAMS (DILBERT). I CAME TO BELIEVE THAT A PRACTICAL KNOWLEDGE OF AS MANY CREATIVE DISCIPLINES AS YOU CAN LEARN IS A VERY GOOD THING FOR YOU AS A CREATIVE VIDMAKER. KNOW FOR YOURSELF YOUR OWN STRENGTHS AND LIMITATIONS, AS WELL AS THE DIFFICULTIES IN VIDMAKING.

I became a filmmaker and then a vidmaker more or less by accident. Ad copywriters were supposed to sit at their typewriters and pound out ideas all day. I started doing experimental commercials and demos to pitch my own ideas. Stop-motion finger painting, wildly arresting graphics, crazy stuff. I was working in *film files,* sticking together an experimental commercial when a lean fellow with a wary look walked in. It was freelance artist reporter Franklin McMahon, Sr., looking for some help making a documentary. Franklin's idea was to follow Presidential candidates around the country, sketching them and taping audio of their speeches. Sound too simple to work? The documentary ran nationally and won us an EMMY AWARD.

SCENE: POLITIC: 68 was shown on WTTW, Chicago, was an election eve NET JOURNAL special and was awarded an EMMY by the Chicago Chapter of the National Academy of Television Arts and Sciences.

The paintings reproduced here were first published by the CHICAGO TRIBUNE MAGAZINE.

PRODUCED AND DIRECTED BY
JACK KLAWITTER

DISTRIBUTED BY
ROCINANTE SIGHT & SOUND
BOX 814
LAKE FOREST, ILL. 60045
PHONE 312/234-9140

Hubert Humphrey at the Conrad Hilton, Chicago

OFFSET SEPARATIONS BY COLLINS, MILLER AND HUTCHINGS, INC.
PAPER; KIMBERLY-CLARK PRENTICE VENETIAN 80#

PRODUCING DOCUMENTARIES WITH FAMOUS AMERICAN ARTIST FRANKLIN MCMAHON, SR. , I CAME TO APPRECIATE THE POWER IN STILLS, IN SKETCHES AND PHOTOGRAPHY. YOU CAN SHOOT PHOTOS WITH YOUR OWN CAMERA, AND USE STILLS TECHNIQUES TO ADD UNIQUENESS AND QUALITY TO YOUR VIDEOS AT A COST YOU CAN AFFORD.

If you've been following any of this, you are starting to realize this isn't brain surgery or rocket science. However, to be a successful maker of your own films or vids, it is important to begin with a clear concept of your world, your idea, the mood you wish to convey. Think again about what Charles and Ray Eames did, and how Franklin McMahon came to create his documentaries. Those people knew the secret to communicating with clarity and conviction is to start with a clear idea of what you are going to do.

HERE I AM DRIVING ONE OF STEVE MCQUEEN'S 'STREET PORSCHE'S ON THE RACE TRACK AT LE MANS, FRANCE. STEVE TOLD ME HE WISHED HIS MOVIE COULD HAVE BEEN MORE LIKE MY DOCUMENTARY ABOUT THE MAKING OF HIS FILM. OF COURSE, IT COULDN'T. STEVE STARTED WRONG, BY SELLING A DRAMA AND THEN TRYING TO PRODUCE A WOODSTOCK-LIKE DOCUMENTARY. HAD HE READ THIS BOOK, THINGS WOULD HAVE GONE BETTER FOR HIM.

You are not creating the *idea* of a vid or a film—*you are about to create an actual world within itself.* So the idea of why you are about to go through this complex and difficult process is important. If money is the only goal, you certainly have to realize that pleasing your client can only carry you so far. What of value can you bring to the table? Is it your fresh and new vision? Your meticulous attention to detail? Your leadership that convinces cast and crew to follow after you through arctic blasts, dank swamps and burning desert sands? Know yourself and know what you want, or you'll always end up making other people's films! Not that vidmaking isn't a team sport…but who owns the team?

What are your opportunities? Video class?
local commercial? Class reunion project?
Upcoming film festival? Geneology?
Some story revealing the corrupt heart of
the city or some unsuppressed evil?
Whatever, write them down.

4 - CLASSIC OR PANTSER?

"The definition of romance is "boy-meets-girl, boy-loses-girl, boy-gets-girl-back" and a Happy Ever After ending."
--Jamie West, Senior Editor, Wild Rose Press

While a definition like the one above is enough to make a true pantser emotionally ill, many modern creative people don't 100% know what they are doing from moment to moment, including many of the successful ones. They peck or paint or video about in a fog. Sometimes that's okay. For instance, if you're continuing a long-running campaign for a frosted breakfast cereal, you need to build a happy thirty second breakfast scene around an anthropomorphically inclined tiger who yells, 'They're Grrrrrreattt!' If you're writing lock-down genre romance, you need only carve the formula into your lower brain functions and go for the sizzle and the sweat. Refer to the quote at the opening of this chapter. If you're painting silk tropical beaches and semi-naked Lady GaGa prints, your path is clear, you don't need a concept. And if you're producing television commercials, just remember the sub-text is always *Buy our product.*

> **YOU MAY BE A PANTSER IF YOU**
> *Believe writers are born, not made.*
> *Are sure outlining is for dummies.*
> *Enable your characters to write*
>   *Their own stories.*
> *Enjoy watching the story fly from*
>   *Your fingertips.*
> *Rant that true art flows from*
>   *Passion, not intellect.*

YOU MAY BE A CLASSIC IF YOU

Lecture structure: beginning, middle, ending, etc.
Revise and rewrite your work until the deadline looms.
Entertain the notions of plot line and character arc.
Don't shrink from words like 'Drama' or 'Comedy'.
Like Tennessee Williams but not William Faulkner.

Even though there are clear formats for writing popular stories, it is easy for the uninitiated or the misguided to fall off the turnip truck into a mud puddle of bad storytelling. If you wish to create one of the many sub-genre types of romance, murder mystery or action adventure, the rules are clear enough. Why then are there a thousand failed manuscripts for every one that is published or produced? One answer is that creative people don't automatically wish to tell stories about what is *popular.* Another is they believe they can be popular *in a fresh new way.*

BOTH C.S. FORESTER AND HERMAN MELVILLE WROTE ABOUT MEN AT SEA, BUT DON'T LET THAT FOOL YOU. FORESTER WAS WRITING ACTION ADVENTURE, WHILE MELVILLE SCRIBBLED A DARK DRAMA ABOUT OBSESSION. ARGUABLY, FORESTER HAD AN EASIER VOYAGE OF IT, WHILE MELVILLE CLIMBED A HIGHER LITERARY MAST. THE MOMENT YOU BEGIN TO WORK UP YOUR FIRST VID, YOU WILL HAVE TO DECIDE FOR YOURSELF: IS IT BETTER TO PRODUCE A WORTHY IDEA OR AN IDEA THAT SELLS BIG TIME? NOT THAT YOU CAN'T DO BOTH. BUT IT MAKES YOU WONDER WHY MORE CREATIVE PEOPLE DON'T DO THAT.

Do-it-yourself vidmaking doesn't have to be complicated as Einstein's theories or far reaching as an episode of Star Trek. Today, because it is possible to produce low budget vids for relatively little money or effort, little shorts in an amazing variety of subjects and styles are appearing every day on internet video websites. I am reminded of the 1960's love generation when tens of thousands of young persons wanted to be potters, folk singers, candle makers and would run around shooting jerky but colorful 16 mm film footage. The potters and candle makers lasted a year or two until the marketplace showed why those crafts had largely died out with the industrial revolution. The bad singers and guitarists were weeded out by their own lack of artistic skills and failure to persist. As for the filmmakers, those who managed to finish one film generally did not attempt a second.

SOMETIMES IT IS YOUR UNIQUE TAKE ON ANY SUBJECT THAT MAKES IT INTERESTING: THIS IS JUST A COMMON CARBONATED BEVERAGE SHOOTING OUT OF A BOTTLE, BUT A QUICK LOOK ON THE INTERNET WILL SHOW YOU HOW MANY PEOPLE WERE INSPIRED TO PRODUCE THEIR OWN VIDEOS AROUND THE SAME SIMPLE CHEMICAL REACTION. [GOOGLE"COKE AND MENTOS MINT EXPERIMENTS"]

When can't you get away with a poor reception for your creative efforts? That one's easy; when you're spending your own time and money. Or when you are creating a video for an important client and you are hoping for repeat business. The dangerous time is after you've written and produced a hit vid; you are numbly gazing at a wall, mulling ideas for your second and everybody is saying what a genius you are, how your very persona radiates *fantastic, sexy and utterly wonderful.* Oh, oh. Dangerous times for the creative mind.

In such perilous moments, a hasty strategic retreat is recommended. Go back to the fundamentals. Re-read this small primer. If that doesn't help, leave at once and recluse yourself to a quiet, unpleasant place like the state penitentiary or a monastery where there are no pleasant distractions. Sit yourself on an uncomfortable chair with your back to the wall and carefully re-read the following books vital to your survival as a creative person:

READINGS TO ENHANCE YOUR NATURAL TALENT:

STORY, by Robert McKee
MAPS OF THE IMAGINATION, by Peter Turchi
EASY READING WRITING, by Peter E. Abresch
MAKING A GOOD SCRIPT GREAT, by Linda Seger
THE ART OF DRAMATIC WRITING, by Lajos Egri
THE SCREENWRITERS WORKBOOK, by Syd Field
THE ART OF THE NOVEL, by Milan Kundera
TINSEL WILDERNESS, by John Klawitter
A BOOK OF FIVE RINGS, by Miyamoto Musashi

If, after reading these instruction manuals, you still feel uncertain about beginning your next creative venture, that is an enormously positive sign. The creative process at its finest is a venture into the unknown, an act of discovery, a journey that becomes a story that you can tell that has a beginning, a middle and an ending.

TAKE A CLOSER LOOK AROUND YOU: EVERYBODY HAS A STORY, AND SOMETIMES IT WILL SURPRISE YOU. SAY YOU'RE OUT THERE DOING A DOCUMENTARY ON STREET BUMS WHEN A COP SHOWS UP AND HANDS THIS GUY A SMALL PAPER BAG. LATER YOU SEE THE SAME BUM SELLING STUFF IN SMALL WRAPPERS TO HIGH SCHOOL KIDS. OH, OH…A REALLY GOOD STORY HAS FOUND YOU.

The success or failure of your project will be determined by the decisions you make at the earliest conceptual moments. Let's say you want to make a documentary style ten minute film titled "A Day In The Life Of A Hollywood Street Bum." This is a project made to order for the pantser style. True, you may start by shooting footage chronologically from the waking hours under cardboard on a park bench when the sprinklers go off, but as a doc vidmaker you have little control over what will happen next.

For doc vidmakers, getting at the heart of the matter is always interesting. A war widow turns out to be a quilter. A meticulous bank clerk moonlights as a Hell's Angel. You never know what you're going to turn up.

The same may be true even if you have your formula down pat and it has proven highly successful for you. Suppose for a moment you are doing short dramatic films of ordinary people going about their daily chores in an unusual or extraordinary way. You'll want your work to be *interesting and have elements of the unexpected.* Even though you are a classic storyteller, in your story the quiet, church going widow seduces the mailman. The old geezer next door takes his twenty year old sedan to Bonneville Flats. The downtrodden cashier at Home Depot decides to rob his own store.

CLASSIC CREATIVES OFTEN FIND THE UNEXPECTED IN THE ORDINARY:
THE RANGE OF HUMAN POSSIBILITES IS SO BROAD THAT *UNUSUAL*
IS NOT PATENTLY ABSURD—BUT THE MORE IMPROBABLE, THE HARDER
YOU HAVE TO WORK TO MAKE IT BELIEVABLE. IN OTHER WORDS, AN 18
YEAR OLD GIRL MAY RUN AWAY WITH A HORNY OLD GEEZER, BUT
CHANCES ARE THEY ARE NOT GOING TO LIVE HAPPILY EVER AFTER.

IDEA #1 FOR VID: HE WAS WAITING WITH MB, HIS THREE YEAR OLD GRANDSON, OUTSIDE APPLEBEE'S. THE PLACE WAS CROWDED, SO HE TOOK MB OVER TO GAWK AT THE ROW OF SHINY HARLEYS. HE ASKED ONE OF THE BIKERS, LOUNGING ON THE LAWN, HOW FAST THEY COULD GO. "PRETTY DAMN FUCKIN' FAST!" THE NEAREST ANGEL REPLIED WITH A ROTTEN TOOTH GRIN. HE DIDN'T THINK AS THE RETORT SHOT BACK OUT OF HIS MOUTH, "HEY, COME ON, HE'S JUST A KID HERE!" THE BIKER FROWNED. "SORRY," HE SAID SHEEPISHLY." THAT *COULD* HAVE HAPPENED, RIGHT? ACTUALLY, IT DID HAPPEN TO MB AND ME.

IDEA #2 FOR VID: LATE ONE NIGHT, GRANDPA WAS ON THE ROAD TO VEGAS WHEN HE HAD A FLAT TIRE. "CRAP," HE SAID, KNOWING HE WAS GOING TO BE LATE FOR HIS POKER GAME. HE COULD ACTUALLY SEE THE LIGHTS OF THE STRIP SHIMMERING IN THE DISTANCE. HE HAD JUST ABOUT FINISHED CHANGING THE DAMN TIRE WHEN A BIKER PULLED UP. "HERE, GRAMPS, LET ME FIX THAT," HE SAID, TAKING THE TIRE IRON FROM THE OLD MAN'S HAND. AN EVIL GRIN LIT THE BIKER'S SCARRED FACE, "YOU SHOULDN'T BE SO TRUSTING." "YOU SHOULD BE MORE DISCERNING YOURSELF," THE OLD MAN SAID, LAUNCHING A DEADLY KARATE KICK AT THE BIKER'S FACE. *NOT VERY LIKELY, RIGHT? YOU CAN SEE RIGHT AWAY THAT IDEA #2, WHILE THEORETICALLY POSSIBLE, WILL TAKE A GREAT DEAL MORE OF A SET UP TO BE BELIEVABLE.*

One way creatives who tell genre stories start their next project is by convincing themselves their video will be totally fresh and new. Of course, it won't be, because the formula is locked in place. But maybe *the situation of the plot* will be new. *The dialogue* (if it is witty and snappy) can be fresh and new. The hero or heroine can be set in *a different location*, given *a new job*, or *a fresh outlook on life*. The novels of thriller writer Dick Francis revolve around some aspect of horse racing. The protagonist is always English, usually in his mid-to-late thirties, usually a retired jockey starting out on some other phase in his life. But occasionally Mr. Francis will throw in a former military intelligence man or member of the British royalty, and his devoted readership often argues about which is the best, the freshest, the most successful of his novels.

Enough about old, dead poets; let's talk about you.
Imagine that you have of late been studying Peter Fonda's road
classic "Easy Rider," and you want to do an improvisational
piece and you are lucky enough to know a couple of young Jack
Nicholsons and Dennis Hoppers who just might be able to pull it
off. Don't kid yourself into believing that's all it takes to pantser
your way through your production. What you will have (or
should be aiming for) is a quasi-structured beginning, middle
and ending. While you will only be able to control the madness
and the blather to some extent, perhaps you can stay
moderately on-point in post production. Still, you should know
beforehand what your story is about. Knowing that, you may be
able to shoot chunks of footage you like and then distill them
into something palatable.

**Thinking further about Easy Rider, the 1960's feature
film:** *What incredible bits of fresh dialogue happen along the
way in that most excellent road picture!* You have to ask
yourself—why don't creatives make more great, wonderful films
and videos exactly like that? In the same vein, why can
seemingly unstructured comics like Robin Williams and, *in
earlier time*s, Jonathon Winters and, *before him*, his royal

hipness, Lord Buckley—why can those geniuses of improvisation do so well at standup comedy and yet their wonderful madness doesn't translate into a great improvisational movie or even a unique short film? If anybody could do improv, like anybody can do the Coke and Mentos thing, wouldn't YouTube be loaded with witty improv vids?

JONATHON WINTERS, CONSIDERED THE MOST WILDLY ORIGINAL IMPROV COMIC OF HIS TIME, HAPPILY TOLD ME (IN THE PARKING LOT OF HANNA BARBERA PRODUCTIONS) THAT HE OWED HIS INSPIRATION TO THE MAD GENIUS OF THE ORIGINAL "DUKE OF HIP", LORD BUCKLEY. AND ROBIN WILLIAMS SAID HE OWED A HUGE CREATIVE DEBT *TO JONATHON WINTERS*. SO MUCH FOR THE HOPEFUL DELUSION THAT THESE PEOPLE RANDOMLY PANTS AWAY IN THE DARK.

Look at us mulling our chances, how to be uniquely creative by following in the footsteps of the greats who have walked before us! How is it that the art of the pantser can be organic and yet involve patterns, flow and designs scouted out by earlier creative minds? Doesn't *pure pantsing* involve going where none have dared go before? Or, look at your situation another way: with millions of ideas and concepts to choose from, *why would you intend to do something pretty much based on the look and feel of Easy Rider?* There has to be a reason.

There are those who will tell you *the art of organic creativity* never works without first firming up structure, form and outline. And they do have a point. Think about the process in terms of creating a fresh and new romance movie, something like "Sleepless in Seattle" or "When Harry Met Sally" (They have similar structures). Once you master the formula, you are free to improvise and you can shift the basics around a bit. Maybe boy-meets-girl, loses girl, gets girl, loses girl and then when all is nearly lost, gets girl again…and then your happy ending.

Oh, crap, you're saying—storytelling can't be this simple as to follow a formula and churn out stories. How could millions of movie goers worldwide be fooled year after year? Well, I didn't mean to imply you simply *imitated*—success comes from *mastering the approach* and then brilliantly executing your own interpretation. Ask yourself about the same concerns in another way—why is it that most movie scripts are 118 pages long, give or take a page or two, or else producers, directors and actors will refuse to read them? Why they are constructed as three act plays? Why are they uniformly ninety to a hundred minutes in length? Why do they tell you at the various Tinseltown Writer's Basic Training Camps that you have to start with an inciting incident and to make sure your first turning point comes on page 29?

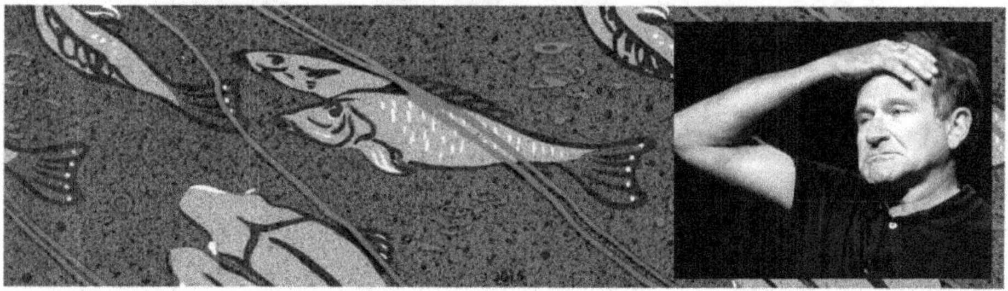

IN THE EARLY 1980'S THE CEO OF DISNEY ASKED WHAT I THOUGHT OF HIS COMPANY CO-VENTURING WITH PARAMOUNT ON "POPEYE", A MOVIE VERSION OF THE STAGE MUSICAL WITH LYRICS BY JULES PFEIFFER AND STARRING ROBIN WILLIAMS AND DIRECTED BY ROBERT ALTMAN. AT THAT TIME, ALTMAN AND WILLIAMS COULD BEST BE DESCRIBED AS TWO OF THE WORLD'S MOST SUCCESSFUL PANTSERS. BUT THERE IS LITTLE ROOM FOR PANTSER-ING WHEN YOU HAVE A LOCK-DOWN SCRIPT WITH PRECISE LYRICS. *HOW MANY WAYS CAN YOU SPELL DISASTER?* THE CEO OF DISNEY DID NOT KNOW THE FUNDAMENTALS NECESSARY TO CREATE A SOLID VISUAL STORY THE WAY I'M TEACHING YOU HERE.

How many times have you heard *You have to play by the rules?* While it is true that an effective short dramatic film or video still needs a beginning, a middle and an end, remember *You are your own vidmaker.* It is your vid and it can be as controversial, wild, crazy, opinionated and sexy as you want, so long as it makes sense, so long as you weave your story well. That's why, if you are going to succeed as a modern *visualizer*, your subject matter, your ideas about life and our times, and your way of presenting what you want to communicate are more important than ever before. I'm sure you can sense what a dangerous game selling out can be. If you warp your idea or your talent just to get it made or sold, you will find yourself locked into a bad idea, a horrible script, a rotten vid tomato bomb.

<u>NOT EVERY HOLLYWOOD PLAYER OR SELF-APPOINTED CRITIC</u> WILL IMMEDIATELY APPRECIATE YOUR GENIUS. BUT YOU DON'T HAVE TO CARE ABOUT THAT. PLAN TO MAKE YOUR VID FOR YOURSELF FIRST. BE STRONG AND TELL YOUR STORY THE WAY YOU WANT. DO IT WELL ENOUGH AND TINSELTOWN WILL BEND TO YOUR GENIUS.

It's time to ponder and finally begin to figure out what kind of vidmaker it is that you think you might be--how much pantser and what degree classic creative? Write down the things you think make you a pantser, and those that mean you are a classic creative.

5 - SELECT A SUBJECT

"Well, most of life is *choices*. If you're going to be successful, you just have to make the right ones."

--Joe Barbera, Co-founder of Hanna-Barbera Productions, home of Yogi Bear, The Flintstones and other cartoon characters..

Successful short stories tend to be about one thing, one illumination, one turning point, and the best ones reflect something important about the human experience. Well, the same can be said about most great short dramatic videos. Let's say you have written a dozen or so really good short stories and you think at least one or two of them might make great little vids. How do you go about selecting?

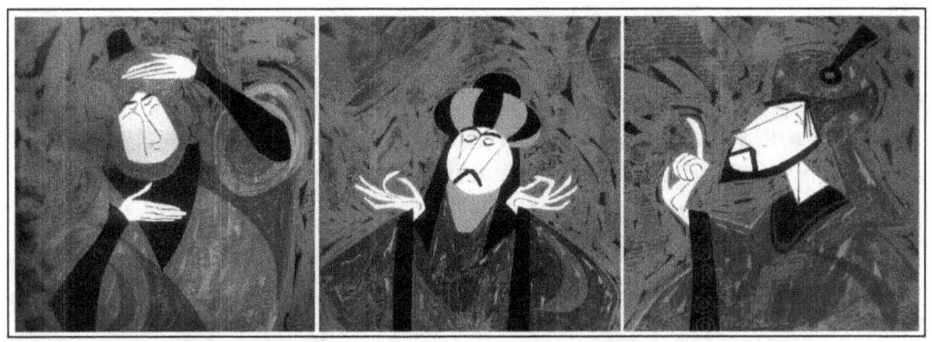

THREE HOPEFUL STORYTELLERS FROM AN ANCIENT AND FAR AWAY LAND SET OUT FOR CAREERS IN BALLADEERING AND MYTHSPINNING. THE FIRST HASN'T ANY TALENT OTHER THAN SELLING HIMSELF, BUT HE HAS A PRINCE AS HIS BACKER AND SO HE HAS LIMITLESS TIME AND MONEY. THE SECOND HAS MORE TALENT THAN THE FIRST AND IS CURRENTLY UNEMPLOYED AND WITHOUT A WIFE AND CHILDREN…AND HE HAS A SMALL INHERITANCE. THE THIRD HAS BY FAR THE MOST TALENT OF THE THREE, BUT HE IS HENPECKED BY HIS THREE WIVES AND HASSLED BY A BROOD OF CHILDREN AND THREE MOTHER-IN-LAWS, TO BOOT. WELCOME TO THE REAL WORLD WHERE YOU MUST EMPLOY EVERY CUNNING STRATEGY TO MAKE THE BEST VIDEO POSSIBLE WITH YOUR AVAILABLE RESOURCES.

When you sit down to write a short visual story, you need the usual tools…a decent computer, or a typewriter or a pencil and a pad of paper—and maybe three or four hours to slap out a first draft. But as you write, you have to be hyper-conscious of The Three Elements of production: **Time, Money and Talent.**

THINGS THAT WILL KILL YOU

Characters – *How many characters do you have in your story? How many main players? How many extras? Do they have to act, that is, know how to emote, or are they action driven stereotypes?*

Location – *Do you have lots of locations? Are they expensive? Are they hard to film? Do you need a specific location?*

Action – *Action scenes are difficult to do right. Car crashes are tricky, car racing is dangerous. The indy producers who did the Gone In 60 Seconds movie owned a car junkyard. You don't.*

Special Effects – *Does your script hinge around explosions or realistic blood effects or violence?*

Special Models – *Do you need that realistic space ship we talked about in an earlier chapter?*

Special Creatures – *How about monsters, Neanderthals or aliens?*

Night Sequences – *Lighting for night sequences can be time consuming and expensive. Are you going to need a generator? Can you get by with the lighting already wired into your interiors?*

Sunset/Sunrise – *Catching the sun going down might be easy, assuming the weather is right…but capturing a just-right lovers' kiss illuminated by the glow of the setting sun might get tricky.*

Aerials – *Expensive and difficult.*

Water – *Expensive, difficult & often cramped quarters.*

Weather – *If your story needs a Tsunami or a tornado, you might want to reevaluate your options. Deserts can be hot, and an evil wind often comes up the moment the sun goes down. Dust plays murder on lenses and camera interiors, and swamp and cave moisture is bad, too.*

Set Design – *You're not really going to want to film in Louis XIV's palace unless you live in France and have lots of Euros.*

Costumes and Clothing – *Everything is cheap until somebody who has it knows you want it.*

Special Make up – *It's hard to keep those vampires looking convincingly bloodthirsty.*

Accidents do happen. They are sometimes marked with a brief credit at the end of a film, actors or members of the crew who lost their lives when a boat flew through the air in an unexpected trajectory or a helicopter dipped into the scene with its killing blades. You are creating the world of your story, and the very process can get out of hand and bring you disastrous consequences. Remember, it's *your* world and *you* are responsible.

1970, LE MANS RACE TRACK. FILMING ACTION SEQUENCES CAN BE DANGEROUS EVEN FOR PROFESSIONAL RACING DRIVERS. IN A PRACTICE RUN, DAVID PIPER TICKED ONE GUARD RAIL, AND THIS PUSHED HIM ACROSS THE TRACK TO SLAM INTO THE GUARD RAIL ON THE OPPOSITE SIDE. THIS FOREGROUND DEBRIS IS ALL THAT IS LEFT OF THE PORSCHE HE WAS DRIVING. DAVID WAS FLOWN TO ENGLAND WHERE HE LOST HIS LEG IN AN OPERATION TO SAVE HIS LIFE. SIR ISAAC NEWTON SAID IT BEST WHEN HE OBSERVED THAT *BODIES IN MOTION TEND TO STAY IN MOTION, AND BODIES AT REST TEND TO STAY AT REST. FRICTION OCCURS WHEN THOSE IN MOTION MEET THOSE THAT ARE NOT.* SEE HOW A SEEMINGLY ABSTRACT PRINCIPLE OF PHYSICS CAN RUIN YOUR BUDGET AND DESTROY YOUR CAREER.

Okay, so *everything* is expensive, complicated and takes lots of time. And filming can be dangerous as well… So we might as well look at this from another angle. The specifics are not as important as your frame of mind. Adapting your idea or your short story to a film becomes manageable once you realize that *some stories are, by their very nature, more difficult to translate to film than others.* If you've got enough time and money (We know you've got the talent.), then, yes, keep those more difficult projects in the mix.

OF THE TWO "GRANDPA & THE BIKER" IDEAS WE TALKED ABOUT IN THE LAST CHAPTER, WHICH DO YOU THINK WOULD BE AN EASIER AND LESS EXPENSIVE SHOOT?

In "Grandpa & The Biker #1", Grandpa and his 3 year old grandson meet a pack of lounging bikers outside an Applebee's restaurant. Immediately you see you're going to need to hire five or ten unruly bikers. You need a three year old, and that can be difficult. And some old 'grandfatherly' fellow who can act, at least a little bit. You're shooting in a parking lot, a busy place with cars coming and going. The bikers are going to want to drink beer and puff weed, which makes the shoot more realistic, but them less manageable. And where are you going to get those bikers in the first place? Overall, an expensive, difficult shoot, even if it is only one location and one day.

In "Grandpa & The Biker #2", you only need one biker and no grandkid. And you can shoot on a lonely roadside somewhere with the lights of Vegas shimmering in the distance. But it's a night shoot, difficult to make look good on film. You think maybe you can solve that by directional lighting, as if it's coming from the headlights of grandpa's car, but the problem there is the lights don't illuminate the area where the flat tire needs to be changed. And you need an old dude who is somehow surprisingly adroit at the martial arts. Guys like that seem easy to find until you need one for your vid. And don't forget, you still need a mean, bad biker.

Both "Grandpa & The Biker" ideas will present problems for the low budget vidmaker. The truth is, no matter what idea you decide to go forward with, the concept you select will present you with production situations that need to be worked out. *How much better then to start thinking production solutions as you write your story idea?* Instead of an Applebees parking lot, maybe Gramps is walking MB past a Harley Davidson shop. And maybe the karate kick scene takes place at a roadside in the daylight hours. And maybe, when all is said and done, these budgetary compromises so water down the ideas that you decide they aren't what you really wanted to say any more. But you recognized that fact early in the process. You are still alive as a vidmaker, ready to find and go forward with a video you know will be true to the visual world you intend to create.

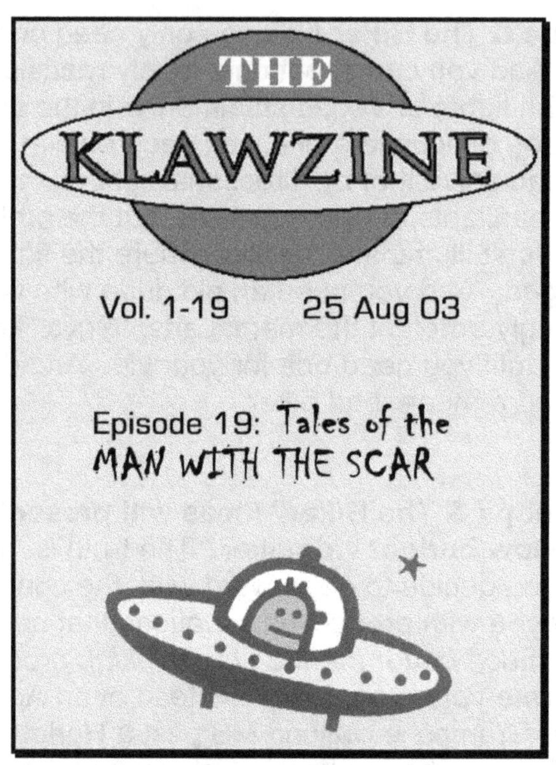

"SPACE ACE," MY SHORT STORY ABOUT PUNKS AND ALIENS, WAS A LOT EASIER TO VISUALIZE ON THE COVER OF MY POPULAR E-ZINE THAN IT WAS WHEN I TRIED TO FIGURE OUT HOW TO SHOOT IT REALISTICALLY AS A LIVE ACTION DRAMATIC SHORT VID.

It helps to start thinking like a vidmaker early on in the process. The point is not that these things are hard to shoot, but rather that some are more difficult than others. Let's take an example or two and work backwards. Consider "Space Ace", my short story about an urban punk who is picked up by aliens and persuaded to spend a few months in farm country, drawing crop signs in the corn and barley fields. Assuming we could create a believable alien or two and dummy up a flying saucer landing, we need multiple night shots with a full moon hanging in the sky to illuminate Ace running through fields of growing grain while dragging a big sled. The conclusion has to be that "Space Ace" is less of a candidate than it might seem at first blush, actually even harder to produce than either of the "Grandpa & The Biker" ideas.

**Let's move on to consider Ernest Hemingway's short
story "My Old Man":** In a poignant tale narrated by the son of
a jockey on the European circuit, we learn the boy travels with
his father. The young lad doesn't say it directly, but we see he
idolizes his dad, as many young men do. The father dies in a
horse race, and much of the story is about what the son learns
in the brief time after the accident, that the father was known to
throw some races, a truth that takes away the boy's innocence.
We could probably shoot this without the thunder and
excitement of the races, but something important would be
missing, and our viewers would sense we produced it on the
cheap. So there's a major money consideration here, plus a
scheduling problem, getting our cast and crew to a race track
somewhere in Europe when the ponies are running. And at
some point we will have to actually create and photograph the
dangerous scene of horses at speed crashing into each other
and the jockey falling to his death, crushed under pounding
hooves. Maybe we could find some old stock footage that

works; maybe not. For something like that, locate the actual
scenes and be sure they work before you commit to the project.

Consider Bret Harte's "All Gold Canyon": A lone
prospector comes across a promising glitter of gold specks
while panning in a stream high in some remote mountains.
Realizing there could be more gold in a nearby hill, he has dug
in over his head when he senses another presence. The
newcomer is a claim jumping intruder who shoots the
prospector. But the prospector only plays dead until the thief
jumps down into the hole. Then the prospector is able to
overcome his assailant and kill him. He digs up all the gold,
buries the intruder in the hole he's dug and leaves. This might
not seem like a good prospect, and it does have its difficulties.
We would need period costumes and a stream in the wilderness
where we could dig around a little—not easy in this age of eco-
awareness. We would also need firearms and some ability to
create a believable struggle on screen. That said, "All Gold
Canyon" might be a prospect if the subject interested us
enough. We only need two actors, a horse or two and a pack
mule. Still, there are weather considerations. And think of the
world of hurt and pain we'd be in if we got to the set and started

to dig that hole next to the stream and then ran into solid rock. Rocks everywhere and we've got actors, crew, two horses and a mule shuffling around and looking at us like we're the world's biggest fools.

I LEARNEDTHE LESSONS I'M TEACHING YOU THE HARD WAY: IN 1983 I OPTIONED FILM RIGHTS TO CHRIS HYDE'S WORLDWIDE BEST SELLING NOVEL, "STYX". I ADAPTED THE BOOK TO SCREENPLAY FORMAT, AND THEN WORKED UP A BUDGET. I LOCATION SCOUTED, AND BEGAN PITCHING TO ANYBODY IN TINSELTOWN WHO WOULD LISTEN. THE PICTURE IS A SURVIVAL THRILLER; A SMALL GROUP OF PEOPLE IS TRAPPED IN A DANGEROUS CAVE SYSTEM. THEIR ONLY HOPE IS TO TRAVEL AN UNDERGROUND RIVER IN A DESPERATE ATTEMPT TO SURVIVE. OVER THREE DECADES LATER, AFTER MANY PITCHES, OPTIONS AND NEAR MISSES, I STILL OWN THOSE RIGHTS AND STILL HAVE NOT PRODUCED THAT FILM. SIMPLY STATED, "STYX" HAS FRIGHTENED OFF EVEN THE MOST EXPERIENCED HOLLYWOOD PROFESSIONALS BECAUSE OF ITS DIFFICULT SETUPS, REMOTE LOCATIONS AND COMPLICATED UNDERGROUND AND UNDERWATER SCENES…THE VERY SCENES THAT MAKE THE PROJECT UNIQUE AND THRILLING.

Once you realize *it's your money you're burning,* you'll get the idea that you must have access to the resources to actually produce and finish your video before you begin. In 2006, I decided to adapt one of my short stories, just like every vidmaker the world over. I was positive and enthusiastic. The time was right; I had lots short stories lying around, and I'd been a *Hollywood Hyphenate*, that is, a writer/producer/director, for decades, most often bringing other people's dreams to life. And I had learned from my adventures in developing "Styx" that I had to be conscious of the immutable production laws of Time, Money and Talent.

<u>THE QUESTION IS NOT WHETHER YOU HAVE GOOD IDEAS</u>. **OF COURSE YOU DO. BUT AS A LOW BUDGET VIDMAKER, YOUR WORLD IS RULED BY THE PRODUCTION EQUATION. CAN YOU ACTUALLY CREATE THE VISUAL REALITY YOU SEE IN YOUR MIND? IF YOU THINK THROUGH THE PROBLEMS AND COMPLICATIONS, AND ARE PERFECTLY HONEST WITH YOURSELF, YOU MAY OR MAY NOT BE ABLE TO GREEN LIGHT YOUR OWN PROJECT. BETTER TO SAY "NO" IN THE FORMATIVE STAGES AND MOVE ON TO A PROJECT YOU CAN DO, RATHER THAN ARRIVE ON LOCATION AND FIND THAT THE PRETTY GIRLS ARE SELF-AWARE, LIBERATED FEMALES NO LONGER WILLING TO DRESS THE WAY YOU IMAGINED.**

My son Matt, who today works at Fox Studios, came to me with a story about a young couple that gets involved in a time-sharing condo offer and finds themselves in the clutches of greedy, enterprising slicksters. Some interesting characters, but loads of meetings with big groups of people. People, of course, mean actors, and no matter how charming and charismatic you are, actors will cost a pile of money. And there's a corollary principle: *The less money you pay them, the more time you have to spend soothing their egos.*

<u>IT IS EASIER TO PRODUCE A SHORT VID</u> FROM AN IDEA THAN FROM A COMPLETED SHORT STORY. BUT IF YOU HAVE A SHORT STORY THAT ABSOLUTELY DEMANDS TO BE ADAPTED INTO A VISUAL REALITY, WHO ARE YOU TO SAY NO TO YOUR MUSE?

I had already rejected dozens of candidates from my own files. I had war stories, show biz stories from my Tinseltown experiences, and MadMen stories from my ad biz days, but I saw with a sinking heart that none of them would suit my purpose. You don't want to mortgage your house, sell your classic Porsche roadster and liquidate your 401k to get in the Santa Barbara Film Festival. So I threw out all the ones that cost too much, needed too much time to film or demanded unique talents and skills that I didn't have. That only left me with a handful to consider. Two or three, truth be told.

I've produced hundreds (thousands, if you count my five year stint as Creative Director at Disney Studios) of short film and video projects…radio, network television, cable, cinema release, TV Commercials, Radio Spots, Marketing Films…as well as long form documentaries, business films, pilots for new shows, television specials…you name it.

But most of those were films using other people's money. I think you'll find that when it's *your vid,* that is, *your* money, *your* time and *your* talent on the line, you'll get a rush purer than anything you've ever experienced.

I thought I had one short story with a timely counter-culture message,* and it seemed we could put a lot of production value up on the screen for relatively little money. It actually only had one human in it, a somewhat naïve lady who goes to the desert on a mission to make the earth a better planet. True, the location was *a desert,* but I live in Los Angeles and the Mojave is nearby…and I figured we would film in the Spring or early Summer when the weather would probably be mild. It was entirely a daytime shoot, with maybe one pick up shot at dusk, and that an easy landscape shot, just the sun going down. *How hard could that be?* Maybe we could even shoot the entire thing in one day. In vidmaking, even an old dog must always beware of the old Latin phrase *ignes fatuus.*

** If you haven't caught on that I'm a dark horse loving, bootstrapping, counter-culture guy, you shouldn't be here.*

IGNES FATUUS, n., *latin.* **FOOLISH PIPE DREAM; SOMETHING THAT MISLEADS OR DELUDES; AN ILLUSION; A PHOSPHORESCENT LIGHT THAT HOVERS OR FLITS OVER SWAMPY GROUND AT NIGHT, POSSIBLY CAUSED BY SPONTANEOUS COMBUSTION OF GASSES EMITTED BY ROTTING ORGANIC MATTER. ALSO CALLED** *FRIAR'S LANTERN, JACK-O'-LANTERN, WILL-O'-THE WISP.*

Write down a list of every possible vid you
believe you want and and actually will be able
to create. Mull, ponder, and finally select
the one or two that you most want to do---
the ones that could work out best for you

6 - FIRST DRAFT

> "Words are, of course, the most powerful drug used by mankind."
>
> *--Rudyard Kipling*

THERE COMES THAT POINT AT WHICH EVERY CREATIVE HAS TO PUT THE GOLDEN WORDS DOWN ON PARCHMENT. HERE'S A STAINED GLASS DEPICTION OF LUKE WORKING ON A FIRST DRAFT OF THE GOSPEL. LOOKS A LITTLE NERVOUS, DOESN'T HE? AT THIS JUNCTURE IN YOUR VID PROJECT, YOU YOURSELF ARE IN A SIMILAR SITUATION, EXCEPT YOU ARE AT A KEYBOARD.

As an eager vidmaker, I'm generally in a rush to get on with the filming. So I have to put the brakes on my inclination to leap forward directly from my rough outline into a shooting script. But I have found over time that, when I overlook the 1st Draft step, I end up going back and rewriting my script a time or twelve. So I like to scribble out a short story first. That way, I can concentrate on feelings, on characterization, on mood and how the action plays out, rather than worry about the realization of the scenes through angles, pans, zooms, cuts, close or long shots, and so on.

The vid I decided to make was "Extinction", a story of an ecology inspired schoolteacher who goes to the Mojave to stop a condo development at the edge of the desert. Some time before I ever thought to make it into a video, I had developed my basic idea into the following short story. It's not very long, just over a thousand words. If you're clear on what you want to say, you can scratch out a workable first draft in one session. Just an hour or two at the keyboard, and you can save yourself days of effort, going back to figure out just what you missed.

<u>Extinction</u>
By John Klawitter

Harley was an ice turtle, the last remnant of a race left behind after the last great ice age. One doesn't think of turtles as adaptable, but as the ice melted and the sun beat down, the same thick shell that had protected him from the freezing snow and polar bear claws now shielded him from the fierce Southern California sun and the snap of the coyote's hungry jaws.

"Hello, there! What have we here?" a voice said. It was Miss Twilliger, on a Sabbatical from the Biology department and involved in contract work for the zoning commission. "Jumping Jiminy, an Ice Turtle!"

"Please, hold it down," Harley said, "I'm catching a few rays and a few Zzzz's here."

"But you're a rare and almost extinct species!" Miss Twillinger trilled.

"You couldn't tell it by me," Harley grumbled, now really annoyed that the newcomer was standing in the early morning sunlight.

"Well, smarty-pants, when's the last time you saw a mating partner?"

"What, a girl turtle? It must have been ten years ago."

"And? And? And?" Miss Twillinger's voice quivered with excitement, hoping she would forthwith be led to a hitherto unknown colony of rare ice turtles.

"And nothing," Harley said. "She was run over by a BMW. Street pizza."

"Oh, what a tragedy for all of nature!"

"Yeah, sometimes life sucks."

The coarse tone of his remark set Miss Twillinger back. Vulgarity didn't seem proper at all, coming from a nearly extinct turtle. He should be grateful he was still around, able to 'suck oxygen', as they say.. Miss Twillinger was a teacher; she felt she could get down with her students and rap street talk with the best of them.

"How old are you, anyway?"

"I'm really old…centuries, maybe even a millennium or two. We ice turtles don't show our age."

"No, you don't look that old," Miss Twillinger agreed.

Harley warily eyed her backpack. He'd been around humans for a long time.

"Say, you're not going to stick me in a bag, are you?"

"No, I'm just doing a survey to see if we should build condos here or not."

"Condos?" Harley tried to scratch his brow but his paw wouldn't reach, so he had to be satisfied with rubbing his head on a nearby boulder.

"Yes, and I'm afraid that wouldn't do. We build condos here, we're going to have to rip up all of this. That would put you out of a home."

"Would they have swimming pools?" Harley was thinking a squat of condos slapped up in his little valley might not be all that bad, what with garbage cans to raid and hot tubs and maybe even a pet cat to snap at.

"Well, yes, probably; but that doesn't matter," Miss Twillinger sniffed. "What matters is that you are an endangered species. We must save you, it is the most important thing."

"Why?"

"Well, mankind has been entrusted with the guardianship of the world, of nature, of everything we see around us."

"By who?"

Miss Twillinger wasn't used to being asked to evaluate her belief system by a lousy, foul-mouthed turtle. She took a swig of designer water from a plastic bottle slung to her hip hugging cargo pants.

"Care for a drink?" she asked.

"Don't mind if I do."

The turtle took a big gulp and then spat it out, "Ugg! No microbes!"

"Of course not. It's the purest water money can buy."

"Don't you find something unnatural in that?"

"Don't be silly. Now, are there other endangered creatures around here?"

Harley nodded his head in a downhill direction, indicated the small dribble that passed for a creek, "Well, we had some little sand fish, but I haven't seen any of them for a decade or so."

Miss Twillinger gasped, "Sand fish! My word! Do you think any of them survived?"

"A few did, but I ate them."

"You should have saved them, to preserve the natural balance."

Harley shrugged, "I was hungry. Oh, how about the yellow stick flower plant? Do plants count?"

"Oh, yes indeed! That would be a very rare find! Could you take me to it?"

Turtles not being very swift of foot, the journey of a hundred yards or so took most of the rest of the day, but just before the sun set, Miss Twillinger was thrilled to see the only example of a yellow stick flower plant, which until now had been considered extinct.

"I like to eat the little yellow flowers," Harley explained, extending his neck and snacking on the closest bud.

"But you mustn't!" Miss Twillinger shrieked. Unfortunately, in her haste to educate the ignorant and ancient turtle, she fell on a sharp boulder next to the creek and badly fractured her left leg, snapping the bone half way between her knee and her foot.

"Help me!" Miss Twillinger wailed.

Harley lifted his heavy shell in an attempt at a shrug, and slowly began to pad away.

"It's not good to hang with the weakest in the pack," he said.

"Pack? There's no pack here."

"Even worse," Harley replied over his shell without pausing or looking back.

"I was going to save you," she cried. "You can't just leave me like this."

His exit, though slow, was inexorable, and after a half hour, Miss Twillinger found she was alone. It was odd, because just over the dark humps of the nearest hills, she could see the glow of the MacDonalds and the Chevron station, and if she listened hard enough, she could make out the relentless hum of drive-time traffic on the freeway.

The pain was intense. She knew her biology; the jagged and exposed edge of bone had cut some vein or other, which would explain all the blood. She had to do something to keep her wits about her. She ran through the chemical chart by heart and recited all the genus and species that she could think of, starting with the invertebrates and ending up with Homo sapiens, and then going back down again through the monkeys and the birds and the amphibians and the fish…she couldn't remember. She swam in and out of consciousness. As darkness descended, she hoped someone would happen by and discover her plight. But she knew that wasn't likely. She remembered how hard she had fought to fence off this small and secluded basin from picnic trash and rutting young lovers who didn't know or even care if they were rolling around on ordinary mustard weed or precious yellow stick flower plants.

Fences, however, meant nothing to the coyotes. They roamed over the hundred and fifty acres she had helped preserve as if it were a playground. And in no time at all, the first coyote showed up. He sniffed at the blood and looked hungrily at the cracked bone sticking out of Miss Twillinger's shin.

"Marrow!" he said, his eyes shining and tongue licking greedily.

YOU HAVE TO BE ON THE LOOKOUT FOR OPPORTUNITY. WE DO HAVE COYOTES ROAMING THE STREETS IN LOS ANGELES COUNTY, BUT THEY ARE CAGY CREATURES, AND YOU'RE NOT GOING TO CAPTURE ONE ON VIDEO, UNLESS MAYBE YOU STAKE OUT YOUR NEIGHBOR'S TOY POODLE.

My choice seems logical, doesn't it? This compact little bit of *flash fiction* has one actress wandering around on the desert, alone except for a tortoise who knows the territory. And there's a quick cameo shot in which a coyote shows up for the ending. *You've read the 1st Draft of "Extinction". See any problems yet?*

Write a rough draft or story outline of the idea or the few ideas you have selected. If you have chosen a short story already completed, you are that much ahead, but now must begin to think visually, to take the next step that leads to translating the spoken word into an audible and visual presentation of your story.

Refer back to the many points listed in this chapter to double-check yourself as to the do-ability of the idea you have selected.

If you are thinking to do a documentary, at this stage you will want to select your direction

If you are doing a commercial, you will want to list and gain approval (from your client) on the copy points that must be handled.

7 - ADAPT IT

"A high and windy bridge is nothing to frighten anyone. Just think of it as a road with no dirt under it. It's all in your point of view, you see…"
--Robert Klavitter, curiosity-driven intellectual and mentor

Some experts will say the word *adapting* with a grand bow of reverence, like it's some really big thing. Well, here's a secret for you. As the writer of your own 1st draft of your story, you already have captured it visually in your head; in fact, you already see it better than anybody else ever will.

<u>MY UNCLE, ROBERT KLAVITTER, (ON THE FAR RIGHT) WINS A BET THAT HE CAN WALK ACROSS THE MISSISSIPPI RIVER</u>

Adapting is just another format, another step closer to actually shooting your vid.. But you are the writer, *you're already all the way there in your head.* Maybe you remember the movie ADAPTATION and the big deal Nicholas Cage made about his psychological turmoil, trying to adapt a novel that was mostly *interior dialogue.* Well, if you have that problem, you've probably picked the wrong concept. Most short vids are about real dialogue and action, not about what anybody might be thinking inside their heads. Yes, actors will give you *nuances* and *interpretations*, but interior dialogue isn't going to win you

the Golden Lion at Cannes or the Silvery Whukka Doodle Doo
in Sidney, Australia.

DO-IT-YOURSELF VIDMAKER TIPS FOR ADAPTATION

If your outline stinks, *so will your screenplay. The chances
are very slim that you can fix it while you're shooting. So get it right
before you move on to the next steps.*

There are no rules *as to how many times you are allowed to
rewrite, so take all the time you need.*

Don't do wordy dialogue. *It will murder your video. If
you're relying on talking heads, you're going to have to pay viewers to
watch your stuff.*

If a scene doesn't move your story forward, kill it.
*Remember, just because you have all the power doesn't mean you
aren't going to make mistakes.*

Write down what works for the director *(in DIY filmmaking,
that is you).*

Don't include anything you'll never be able to shoot.
*Reaching for a shot that is beyond your means opens you to critical
scorn and financial ruin.*

**Don't consider your outline or original material to be a
sacred cow.** *If you find a better idea, go with it. If that makes you a
pantser, learn to live with the (totally self-imposed) scorn and shame.*

Remember, a script is a story *written for a special purpose—
to be produced.*

Forget all that crap about writing pitch lines *for lazy
professional producers. You are your producer, your director, your
own boss.*

'

Okay, what is sub-text? Purists will tell you this is a subject
best left to directors, but that is rubbish. You have to start
thinking *internal motivation* the very minute you decide to write
and adapt your own material. Sub-text is *What do the words*

really mean? The sub-text of all television commercials is simply *Buy this product.* I mention sub-text at this point not only because you have to be the master of your characters and their motivations, but because directors and actors often want to interpret your story in ways that contradict your original meaning. And—surprise!—as you adapt your story you, yourself, may find reason to revise, enrich or shift what you want to say. Hell, it's your story. If you come to feel a character has deeper or in some way better meaning when interpreted a different way from the original, so be it. But don't allow anybody else to re-interpret it for you.

<u>WHY IS SPONGE BOB SQUARE PANTS SO ENTERTAINING?</u> WHAT MAKES THE EPISODES ON HIS SHOW CLICK FOR SO MANY AGE GROUPS? HOW IS IT THAT VIEWERS ACCEPT PHYSICALLY IMPOSSIBLE REALITIES WITHOUT A SECOND THOUGHT, BUT WHEN IT IS THE WORLD OF YOUR OWN CREATION THEY ARE UNWILLING TO SUSPEND THEIR DISBELIEF? TO BE LIKE SPONGE BOB, YOU SHOULD AIM FOR A COMPLETELY THOUGHT OUT WORLD OF YOUR OWN CREATION, AND FOR FLAWLESS EXECUTION. YOUR GOAL IS TO ENCOURAGE BELIEVABILITY. THE WORLD OF BIKINI BOTTOMS IS, YOU SEE, TOTALLY THOUGHT OUT AND LOGICAL *IN ITS OWN CONTEXT*. THIS IS WHY SPONGE BOB AND PATRICK CAN BLOW BUBBLES UNDER WATER, AND BOAT-CARS FLOAT OVER THE SEA BOTTOM, AND SQUIDLY PLAYS THE CLARINET—AND VIEWERS NEVER GIVE ANY OF THE TWISTED LOGIC A SECOND THOUGHT.

If you want to create a technically flawless script, buy screenwriting software like Final Draft. It will cost you a hundred bucks or so, but you'll never have to worry that some producer is going to reject your script because you said SUNRISE before you said EXTERIOR. Oh, wait. You *are* the producer, so if you don't want to blow a C-note, just use Microsoft Word. You'll have to learn to indent your dialogue and center up who is speaking, but it's only ten or twenty pages and I'm assuming you are tenacious and learn fast.

How about camera directions? Maybe you've heard some directors are offended when you suggest a wide angle shot of a panoramic scene, or zooming in to feature blood running from multiple stab wounds. Oh, wait again—you *are* the director. It would seem the best technique would be to put in as many directions as you will want to refer to later under the glare of the lights and in the heat of the moment, when you are actually filming.

So you adapt it and you look at it and maybe it is okay, but maybe you yourself have a dreaded sinking feeling in your creative innards. So you rewrite it a time or two until it feels right. One thing you recognize right away is that when you are writing in your own story world, in a 1ˢᵗ Draft a sense of time inside the story can be handled, finessed or cheated in a dozen different ways. But in the adaptation, time marches on like a robot. That means *your sense of timing* becomes important in a new way. Things you thought funny in your short story now seem dull or wordy. Things you thought were snappy are now vague and meaningless. It's a great discipline, adaptation. While adapting my novels to screenplays, I learn so much about my characters and their stories that I generally go back and rewrite the novel. But that's another how to book, if I survive writing this one and live long enough to get to it.

After various drafts, my script adaptation of "Extinction" looked like this:

```
EXTINCTION screenplay R6


OPEN CLOSE ON A COMMON, ORDINARY LOOKING
DESERT TORTOISE.
The TORTOISE, whose name is HARLEY, is slowly
making its way on an asphalt road.  We hear an
approaching car, and it passes by.

We hear a dramatic squeal of brakes and rubber
on the road, and wheels flash by, missing
Harley by what looks like inches.

Unperturbed as only a tortoise can be, Harley
continues.

Another car, another squeal, another near
miss, this time by a motor bike wheel that
actually drives between Harley and the camera.

Harley again continues.
Harley awkwardly makes his way off the
asphalt.

Harley thumps into a weedy roadside field.
```

Various angles as Harley slowly but inexorably
passes by fast food wrappers and soda pop cans
and rubber prophylactics, all thrown out the
windows of passing cars over the past weeks
and months and years.

Harley pads into an area where there is some
vegetation, rocks, barren land.

As we watch his progress away from the road,
we hear the calm voice of a NARRATOR. This
voice is somewhat like the male narrator in
American Dream, but with the confident bemused
voice of the female narrator in Desperate
Housewives.

NARRATOR (V.O.)
Harley was an ice turtle, a tortoise,
actually, the very last remnant of a race of
shelled creatures left behind after the last
great ice age. One doesn't think of turtles
as adaptable, but as the ice melted and the
sun beat down, the same thick shell that had
protected him from freezing snow and polar
bear claws now shielded him from the fierce
sun and the snap of the coyote's hungry jaws.

MISS TWILLINGER (V.O.)
Hello! What have we here?

ANGLE ON MISS TWILLINGER
She is in her late 30's, plain-faced, lean and
healthy looking. She is a nature lover on a
day hike and she is dressed appropriately so
in snappy hiker's attire that is common tan
but well-pressed and clean. She has a day
pack strapped to her back and bottled water at
her belt.

Her hustle & bustle irritates Harley, who can
talk

HARLEY
(Bored, irritated) Please hold it down, I'm
trying to catch a few Zee's and a few rays
here...

MISS TWILLINGER
My Gracious, an Ice tortoise!

HARLEY
(complaining) Come on, you're in my light.

MISS TWILLINGER
But you're a rare and almost extinct species!

HARLEY
You couldn't tell it by me.

Miss Twillinger is a teacher; she takes no crap
from anyone, particularly not some other
species way down the food chain. And she knows
how to get to a turtle who is almost extinct.

MISS TWILLINGER
Grumpy, aren't you? When's the last time you
bumped beaks with a mating partner?

HARLEY
What, a sweet-lipped girl turtle? (he thinks
about it) Must have been ten years ago.

This arouses Miss Twillinger's interest. Maybe
there's a little brood of this nearly extinct
animal nearby.

MISS TWILLINGER
And? And? And??!!

HARLEY
And nothing. She was run over by a BMW 530i.
Street pizza.

MISS TWILLINGER
My God, what a tragedy for all of nature!

HARLEY
Yeah. Sometimes life sucks.

Miss Twillinger eyes him, a frown on her face,
and she shakes her head. She is not at all
pleased with his manner.

MISS TWILLINGER
You should be grateful you're still around,
'sucking oxygen' as my students say...how old
are you, anyway?

HARLEY
I'm really old. Centuries, maybe even a
millennium or two. We don't show our age much.

MISS TWILLINGER
You don't look that old.

Harley warily eyes her backpack.
HARLEY
Say, you're not going to stick me in that
backpack, are you?

MISS TWILLINGER
No, I'm just part of a survey to protest the
new condos they want to build here.

HARLEY
Condos?
Harley rubs his head against a nearby rock.

MISS TWILLINGER
Yes, and I'm afraid that will not do. We build
condos here, we have to rip all this up. That
puts you out of a home.

WIDE SHOT OF THE VALLEY.
It is sparse and scrubby, rocky and maybe even
has some cactus.

Harley looks around skeptically
HARLEY
Would they have swimming pools?

MISS TWILLINGER
Yes, probably, but that doesn't matter.

HARLEY
And garbage cans? There's nothing wrong with a
garbage can raid, long as you don't fall in.

MISS TWILLINGER
What matters is that you are an endangered
species. We must save you, it is the most
important thing.

HARLEY
Why?

Miss Twillinger gives him a superior look.

MISS TWILLINGER
Did all that ice addle your brains? Mankind
has been entrusted with the guardianship of
the world, of nature, of everything we see
around us.

HARLEY
By who? Oh, sorry, 'whom'?

Miss Twillinger is not used to being asked to
evaluate her belief system by a lousy, foul-
mouthed turtle. She frowns at him without
speaking, and then takes a swig of designer

water from a plastic bottle slung to her hip
hugging knee length cargo pants.

MISS TWILLINGER
Care for a drink?

HARLEY
Don't mind if I do.
The turtle takes a drink, gags and spits it
out.

HARLEY
Jesu Christi Morris! No microbes.

MISS TWILLINGER
Of course not, it's the purest water money can
buy.

HARLEY
Don't you find something unnatural in that?

Miss Twillinger's frown deepens. She
impatiently looks around.

MISS TWILLINGER
Don't be silly. Now, are there any other
endangered creatures around here?
Harley nods his head in the downhill
direction, indicating the small sandy dribble
that passes for a creek.

HARLEY
Well, we had some little sand fish, but I
haven't seen any for a decade or so.

MISS TWILLINGER
Sand fish! My word! Do you think any of them
survived?

HARLEY
A few did, but I ate them.

Miss Twillinger angrily slams her water bottle
back in its custom socket.

MISS TWILLINGER
That's exactly what I'm talking about, you
greedy little tortoise! You should have saved
them, to preserve the natural balance.

HARLEY
Come on, I was hungry...Oh, how about the
yellow stick flower plant? Do plants count?

MISS TWILLINGER
Why, why yes! That would be a very rare find!
Could you take me to them?

HARLEY
Sure, but I'm not very swift of foot.

Angles on Miss Twillinger following the
turtle. He leads her down the valley, not
very far, but through cross dissolves and
lengthening shadows, we get the idea the day
is passing.

Angle on a plant with little yellow flowers.
Harley and Miss Twillinger approach it.
Harley extends his neck and takes a snack of
some of the flowers.

HARLEY
I like to eat the little yellow flowers.

Miss Twillinger loses her wits completely and
lunges to stop Harley.

MISS TWILLINGER
No!! you mustn't!!
In her haste to educate the ignorant and
ancient turtle, Miss Twillinger falls on a
boulder next to the creek.

There is a sharp, snapping sound.

MISS TWILLINGER
Owwwwww!

Miss Twillinger's leg is fractured and bloody,
and worse, her other leg is caught under a
boulder.

MISS TWILLINGER
My God, My God, the pain! Help me!

Harley silently looks at her.

MISS TWILLINGER
I'm stuck, I can't get out of here!

Harley continues to look at her, saying
nothing.

MISS TWILLINGER
Say something, do something! Oh, my God, my
God, my God!

As she wails in misery, Harley turns and
slowly begins to pad away.

MISS TWILLINGER
Wait! Where are you going?

Without turning, the retreating Harley talks
over his shoulder.

HARLEY
It's not good to hang out with the weakest in
the pack.

MISS TWILLINGER
Pack?! There's no pack here!

Harley doesn't pause or even look back.

HARLEY
Even worse.

MISS TWILLINGER
I was going to save you! I was going to save
you!

The sun has set. Miss Twillinger is left
alone in the twilight. She is in obvious
agony. Blood oozes from her fractured leg.

NARRATOR
Harley the ice tortoise's exit, though slow,
was inexorable, and after a half hour Miss
Twillinger found she was alone. The pain was
intense. She knew her biology; the jagged and
exposed edge of bone had cut some vein or
other. She had to do something to keep her
wits about her.

NARRATOR (CONT)
She recited all the genus and species that she
could think of, starting with the
invertebrates and ending up with Homo sapiens,
and then going back down again through the
monkeys
and the birds and the amphibians and the
fish...she couldn't remember any more...She
was swimming in and out of consciousness. She
felt the oddness of it all because just over
the dark humps of the nearest hills, she knew
there was a MacDonalds and a Shell station.
Still, it was certain that nobody was coming.
They had fenced this area off particularly to
keep out the trash and the rutting young
lovers who didn't know or even care if they
were rolling around on ordinary mustard weed
or precious yellow stick flower plants.

A dark figure against the sunset, we see a
coyote.

```
NARRATOR (CONT.)
Fences, however, meant nothing to the coyotes.
The thousand or so acres she had helped
preserve was their playground, their
sanctuary, their home.

Closer on the coyote.
Closer still.

Really close.  His eyes gleam.  He pants, we
see his teeth, a sort of grin.  His tongue
licks greedily.
COYOTE
Bone marrow!
The coyote starts down the hill, heading for
Miss Twillinger at a steady trot.

Sunset dims to blood red, and then to black.
Credits over

END
```

You finally get a draft you like enough to move forward. Maybe by now it is days or weeks later, but you're itching to *roll film,* or as they say these days, *start video.* But wait yet again; there's a chance you might not be ready for all that action. Take a page from great directors like Alfred Hitchcock and Norman Jewison. Those luminaries never walked on a set without their storyboard, the visual representation of what they think they might like to put on the screen. A storyboard for a screenplay is a thick volume of visuals that helps them focus their concentration on the task ahead. Such preplanned visuals save time, too, when you're on the set, burning money by the minute.

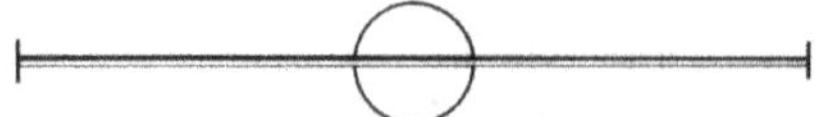

Adapt the outline or short story you have selected
to script format. If you don't know what that's
like, you can pick up the idea on the internet.
There's no big secret to it, and they are all the same.
You establish a scene as to location and time of day.
You describe action. You add dialogue.

The key to adapting is to pretend you are translating
your story for an idiot, that is, the film director.
You can be politically correct with this as the idiot
is you since you most probably will be directing.

Think visually. Remember, the transitions between
scenes are important. Not that you have to add
directions like zooms and fades at this moment...
just keep in mind the flow of action. You are telling
a story with pictures as well as words. A heady
brew, but you're up to the task. Same story, you see...
just a different format. So get at it.

8 - STORYBOARD IT

"I don't need to draw good. I see it in my head."
--Nameless young art director, Grey Advertising.

You don't have to know how to draw really well to sketch out your storyboard. Many art directors, of course, have talented wrists, but many others get by on stick figures and *chutzpah*. They'll tell you *This is my visualization, I don't have to draw good.* And, in this case, they are right. Your viewers, the people who will see your finished vid, will never see any of your crude little sketches. You draw them to remind yourself of camera angles, of zooms and pans, of the way your inner mind sees the unfolding of your story. You wouldn't use such a storyboard to impress big money investors, but you don't want to blow thousands of dollars on a finished storyboard when some scratchy little sketches will accomplish the same trick for you.

IN WORKING UP MY STORYBOARD FOR "EXTINCTION", NOTING THE SIZE RELATIONSHIP BETWEEN MISS TWILLINGER AND THE TURTLE (LOWER SCREEN RIGHT) BEFOREHAND ENABLED ME TO PLAN OUT MY SHOTS, SAVING VALUABLE TIME WHEN ACTUALLY ON THE SET. THIS WAS IMPORTANT, AS DESERT TORTOISES CAN NOT SPEND MORE THAN SIXTY SECONDS IN THE SUN WITHOUT BEGINNING TO COOK IN THEIR SHELLS.

On the payroll (or at least on retainer) at big ad agencies across the U.S. and working for studios and production companies out here in Tinseltown, there are art directors whose everyday work is so excellent it sometimes is framed and hung on walls. These storyboards are not only of value to the director, they are often important to clients and investors who are dumping down a pile of money (often seven or eight figures for a 30 or 60 second commercial) or millions for a blockbuster movie and want to be charmed and romanced a little bit as to the value of the idea to which they are committing. As an agency producer, I would sometimes translate the storyboard stills to a camera-moves-on-artwork video. And sometimes even that wasn't enough to impress a client.

HERE'S A FRAME FROM A STORYBOARD I HAD CREATED FOR A DISNEY MOTION PICTURE, "A WIND TO THE WEST", BASED ON A BOOK ABOUT AN EAST GERMAN FAMILY THAT STITCHED TOGETHER A BALLOON IN A BRAVE ATTEMPT TO FLY ACROSS THE BORDER DURING THE COLD WAR. ALAS, THE DECISION MAKERS DECREED MY IDEA WAS TOO *'POETIC'*, AND THE PROJECT NEVER GOT BEYOND THE STORYBOARD STAGE.

You try to visualize what the camera sees. Your storyboard is a way of thinking, of capturing the essence of the moment at the moment it is being shot—and, as important, what you as the writer saw in your genius moment of creative madness. No matter if your wrist is shakier then Thurber's or more primitive than the guy who draws Dilbert, you can do this.

HERE'S A FRAME I DREW FOR A KAISER PERMANENTE HEALTH CARE PROJECT. MY PITCH TO DO THE TELEVISION COMMERCIALS WENT DOWN IN FLAMES, AND MY COMPANY DID NOT GET TO PRODUCE THE TELEVISION SPOTS, BUT THE KP PEOPLE PAID ME GOOD MONEY FOR THIS HORRIBLE SKETCH AND USED IT IN A BROCHURE THEY SENT OUT IN A MASS MAILING TO MILLIONS OF THEIR HEALTH CARE CUSTOMERS.

You can do your own storyboard. Don't let anybody talk you out of it. Who better than the writer, the one who first brought the story to life? Believe me, if I can do it, you can do it. And you don't need a professional's knowledge of lenses and camera moves. Anybody who watches movies knows what the shot looks like when seeing what E.T. sees or what it looks like when a vampire flies in the window or a band of half-human wolves streak across the forest at super-speed. But those viewers are never going to see your storyboard. Since you are going to be directing, you are basically pre-planning your on-set thinking. In short, only you have to know what the scratchy sketches stand for. So just sketch it out any way you want, so long as you understand what your thinking is. Your work doesn't have to look like Rembrandt or Hockney; you just have to recognize in your sketch what you intend to capture in the frame. Believe me, you'll thank me on the set when confronted with blank stares from the cast and crew, everybody waiting for your unique vision of the next shot.

I did not have a storyboard when I sold the script I wrote for "The Navajos Water The Desert. When shooting documentary style, it is not always possible to visualize exactly what you are going to film. I felt my script was solid because I had a good Navajo friend, Jimmy Shorty, who worked as a hydrologist for the tribe. But once I got there I wished I'd preplanned the visuals. It could have saved me time and energy, and I undershot some scenes and later wished I'd had more coverage.

NAVAJO RESERVATION, NORTHERN NEW MEXICO. THERE WAS NO WAY TO KNOW BEFOREHAND THAT OUR WATER RIG WOULD BE HELD UP BY AN OLD NAVAJO ON HORSEBACK. THAT WATER RIG BURNS TWO GALLONS OF GASOLINE EVERY MILE, AND WE HAVE 150 MILES TO GO. THAT'S ME FOLLOWING IN THE FORD BRONCO DIRECTLY BEHIND THE WATER RIG, AS THE REST OF THE CREW BRINGS UP THE DUSTY REAR.

"THE NAVAJOS WATER THE DESERT", HANNA-BARBERA PRODUCTIONS.
WHEN YOU SHOOT DOCUMENTARY LOW BUDGET STYLE, SOMETIMES THE
WRITER/DIRECTOR (ME) DRIVES THE CAR AND THE PRODUCER (DAN
ELLITHORPE) IS THE CAMERAMAN. AND WHEN EVERY MINUTE COUNTS,
YOU ARE VERY HAPPY TO HAVE A STORYBOARD TO GUIDE YOU.

We were able to get the water rig down a steep and narrow
road onto Monument Valley. Quick-thinking Jimmy Shorty, the
Navajo geologist, had to jump out of one of the jeeps and stick
rocks under the wheels as it started to slide over the steep edge
of the gravel road. But he was able to stop it on the brink of
disaster and we ended up getting great footage.

Just what does it take to do a storyboard? World famous artist Franklin McMahon, Sr. told me he needed a Number 2 HB pencil and a little canvas chair set on a busy street corner and he would be able to record the world passing by. In his documentary "The Artist As A Reporter", he does a convincing job of showing how his sketches and drawings can be used to create films that capture the feeling and imagery of times gone by. I worked on that seminal documentary, as well as producing and directing several others with him, and that was how I acquired some of my ideas about storyboarding. I soon realized that, unlike Franklin's drawings, most storyboards never see the light of day. They are helpful because, as a director—whether on location or on a set—you must work efficiently. All that said, I'll go further and prove it to you. On the next pages, in its rough and ready reality, is my crude but efficient storyboard for my short dramatic film "Extinction", produced in 2006:

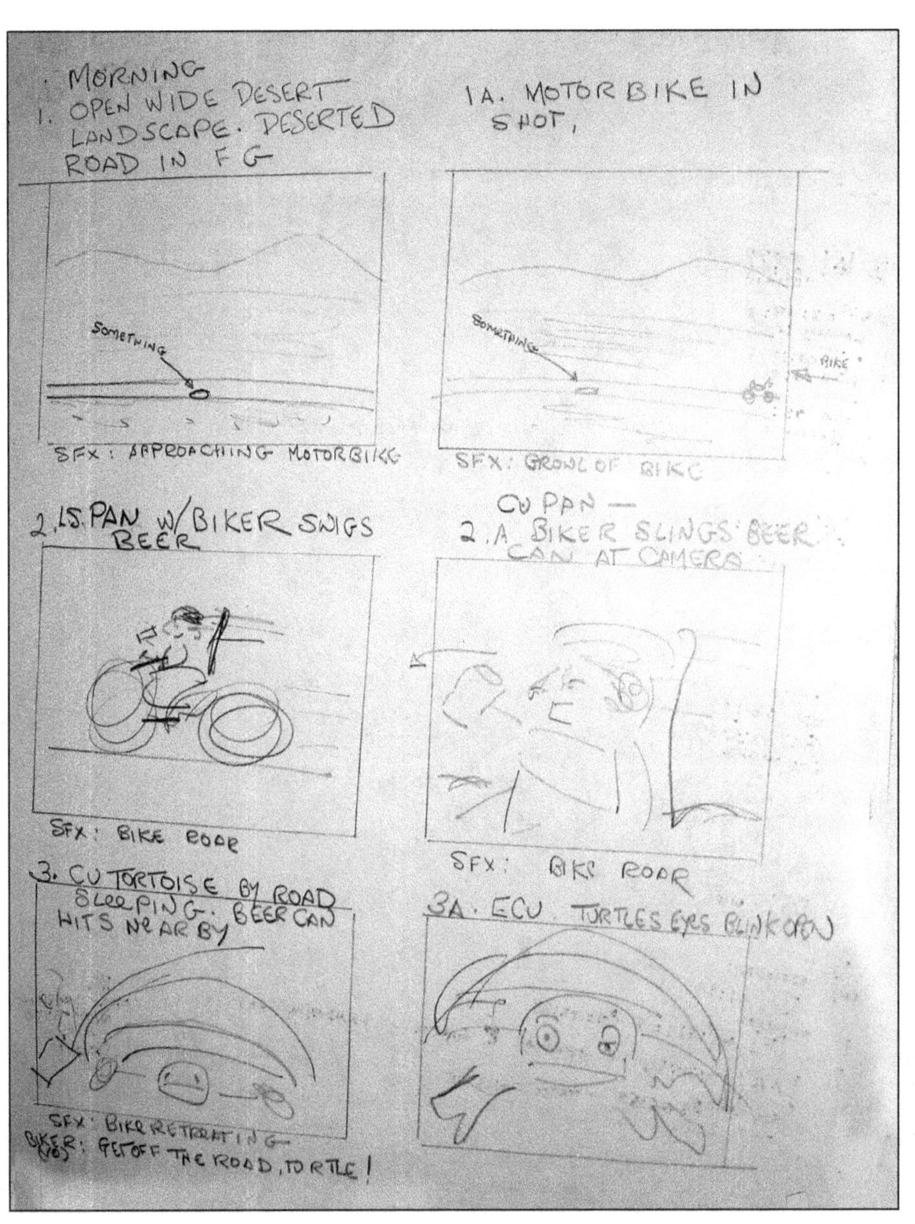
· MORNING
1. OPEN WIDE DESERT
LANDSCAPE. DESERTED
ROAD IN F.G.

SOMETHING

SFX: APPROACHING MOTORBIKE

1A. MOTORBIKE IN
SHOT.

SOMETHING

BIKE

SFX: GROWL OF BIKE

2. LS. PAN w/BIKER SWIGS
BEER

SFX: BIKE ROAR

CU PAN —
2.A BIKER SLINGS BEER
CAN AT CAMERA

SFX: BIKE ROAR

3. CU TORTOISE BY ROAD
SLEEPING. BEER CAN
HITS NEARBY

SFX: BIKE RETREATING
BIKER: GET OFF THE ROAD, TURTLE!
(VO)

3A. ECU TURTLES EYES BLINK OPEN

4. REVERSE ANGLE: TURTLE SCUTTLES AWAY OFF ROADSIDE

5. FRONT ON TURTLE MAKING WAY THROUGH ROADSIDE DEBRIS

PHIL D

NARR. (VO): HARLEY WAS AN ICE TURTLE, A TORTOISE, ACTUALLY. THE VERY LAST REMNANT OF A RACE OF SHELLED CREATURES LEFT BEHIND AFTER THE LAST GREAT ICE AGE

6 SIDE ANGLE - TURTLE - ROADSIDE

A MATT+JOHN KLAWITTER FILM
EXTINCTION
DEL TACO

7. FRONT ANGLE TURTLE - ROADSIDE JUNK THINGTING

PRODUCED BY MATTHEW KLAWITTER

NARR (VO): ONE DOESN'T THINK OF TORTUS AS ADAPTABLE BUT AS THE ICE MELTED AND THE SUN BEAT DOWN

8 ANGLE ON HARLEY LEAVING ROADSIDE

WRITTEN + DIRECTED BY JOHN KLAWITTER

NARR (VO): THE SAME THICK SHELL THAT HAD PROTECTED HIM FROM FREEZING SNOW AND POLAR BEAR CLAWS...

9. HARLEY NOW ON TRUE DESERT

AT END OF SHOT, MISS TWILLINGERS SHADOW ACROSS HIS SHELL

STARRING
HEIDI CAITLIN

NOW SHIELDED HIM FROM THE FIERCE SUN AND THE SNAP OF THE COYOTES HUNGRY JAWS.

MISS TWILLINGER (VO): HELLO! WHAT HAVE WE HERE?

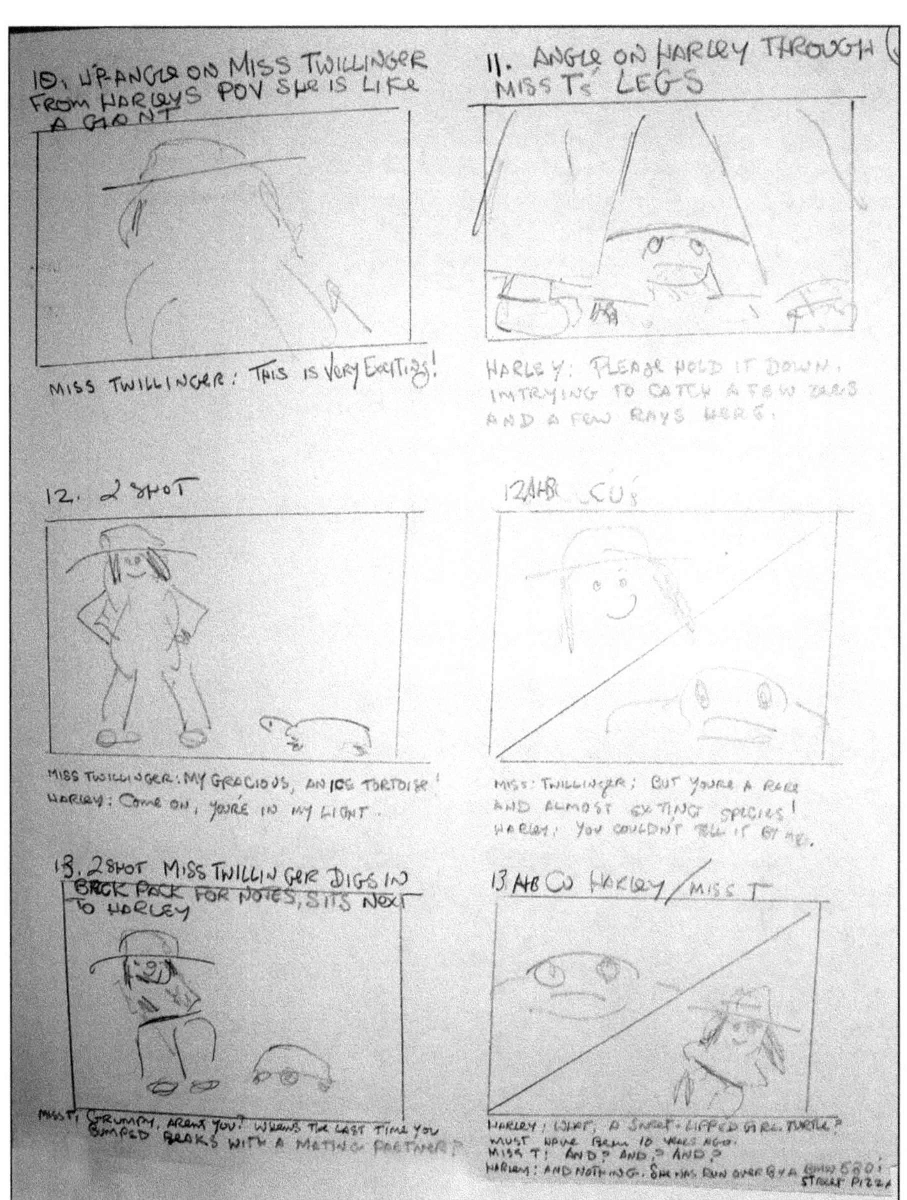

10. ¾ ANGLE ON MISS TWILLINGER FROM HARLEYS POV SHE IS LIKE A GIANT

MISS TWILLINGER: THIS IS VERY EXCITING!

11. ANGLE ON HARLEY THROUGH MISS T's LEGS

HARLEY: PLEASE HOLD IT DOWN. I'M TRYING TO CATCH A FEW ZZZS AND A FEW RAYS HERE.

12. 2 SHOT

MISS TWILLINGER: MY GRACIOUS, AN ICE TORTOISE!
HARLEY: COME ON, YOU'RE IN MY LIGHT.

12A HB CU'S

MISS TWILLINGER: BUT YOU'RE A RARE AND ALMOST EXTINCT SPECIES!
HARLEY: YOU COULDN'T TELL IT BY ME.

13. 2 SHOT MISS TWILLINGER DIGS IN BRCK PACK FOR NOTES, SITS NEXT TO HARLEY

MISS T: GRUMPY, AREN'T YOU? WHENS THE LAST TIME YOU BUMPED BEAKS WITH A MATING PARTNER?

13 AB CU HARLEY/MISS T

HARLEY: WHAT, A SNOUT-LIPPED GIRL TURTLE? MUST HAVE BEEN 10 YEARS AGO.
MISS T: AND? AND? AND?
HARLEY: AND NOTHING. SHE HAS RUN OVER BY A BMW 520: STREET PIZZA

13. TWO SHOT

MISS TWILLINGER: MY GOD, WHAT A TRAGEDY FOR ALL OF NATURE!
HARLEY: YEAH, SOMETIMES LIFE SUCKS

13C CU MISS T's DISAPPROVAL

MISS T: YOU SHOULD BE GRATEFUL YOU'RE STILL
AROUND, "SUCKING OXYGEN" AS MY STUDENTS SAY...
HOW OLD ARE YOU ANYWAY?

13D VERY WIDE SHOT, NOTHING AROUND THE TWO OF THEM BUT DESERT

HARLEY: I'M REALLY OLD. CENTURIES, MAYBE
EVEN A MILLENNIUM OR TWO. WE DON'T
SHOW OUR AGE THAT MUCH.
MISS TWILLINGER: YOU DON'T LOOK THAT OLD.

13A CU HARLEY

HARLEY: SAY, YOU'RE NOT GOING TO
STICK ME IN THAT BACKPACK, ARE YOU?

13B. CU MISS TWILLINGER

MISS T: DON'T BE RIDICULOUS. I'M JUST PART OF A
SURVEY TO PROTEST THE NEW CONDOS
THEY WANT TO BUILD HERE

13D VERY WIDE SHOT

HARLEY: CONDOS?
MISS T: YES, AND I'M AFRAID THAT WILL NOT DO.
WE BUILD CONDOS HERE, WE HAVE TO RIP
ALL THIS UP. THAT PUTS YOU OUT OF A HOUSE.

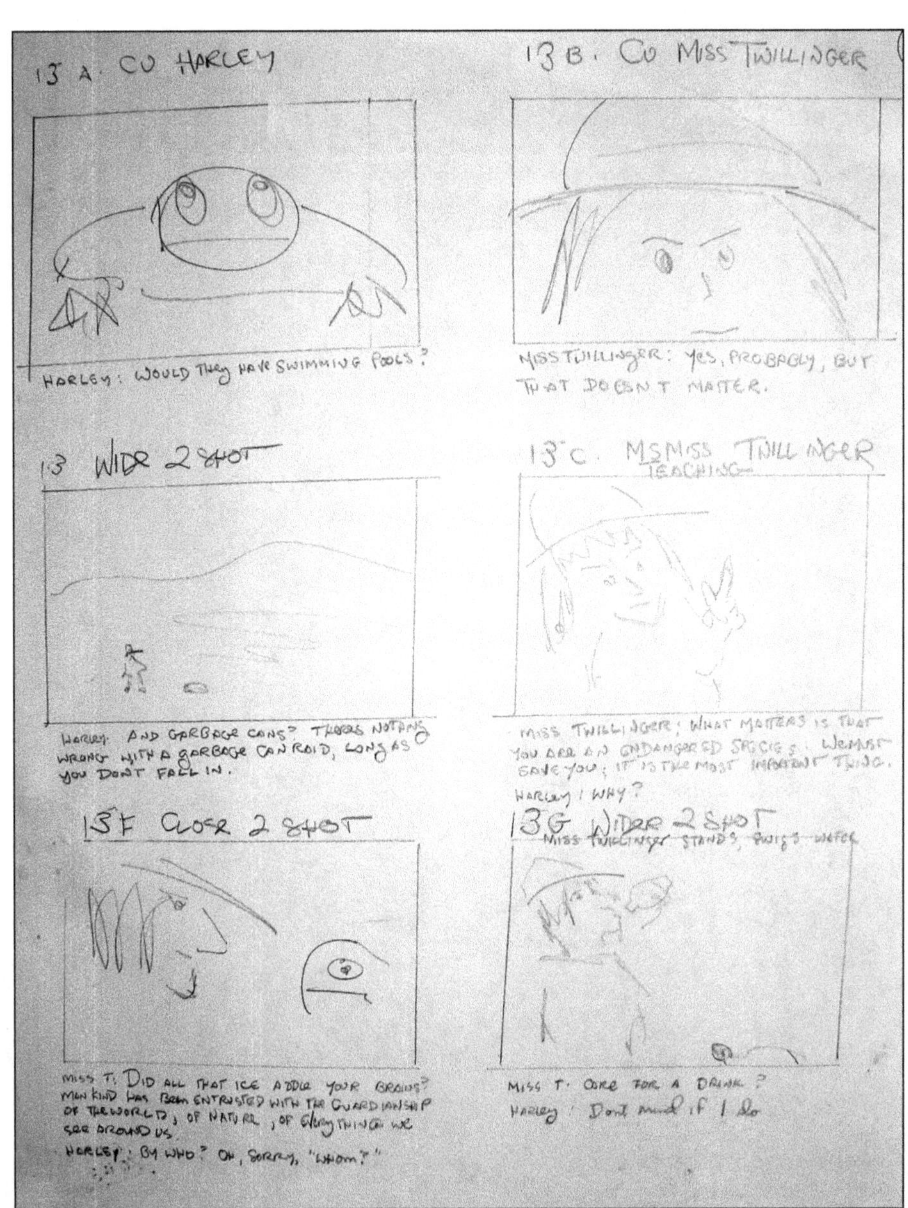

13 A. CU HARLEY
13B. CU MISS TWILLINGER
HARLEY: WOULD THEY HAVE SWIMMING POOLS?
MISS TWILLINGER: YES, PROBABLY, BUT THAT DOESN'T MATTER.
13 WIDE 2 SHOT
13 C. MS MISS TWILLINGER TEACHING
HARLEY: AND GARBAGE CANS? THERE'S NOTHING WRONG WITH A GARBAGE CAN ROID, LONG AS YOU DON'T FALL IN.
MISS TWILLINGER: WHAT MATTERS IS THAT YOU ARE AN ENDANGERED SPECIES. WE MUST SAVE YOU; IT IS THE MOST IMPORTANT THING.
HARLEY: WHY?
13F CLOSE 2 SHOT
13G WIDER 2 SHOT
MISS TWILLINGER STANDS, POURS WATER
MISS T: DID ALL THAT ICE ADDLE YOUR BRAIN? MANKIND HAS BEEN ENTRUSTED WITH THE GUARDIANSHIP OF THE WORLD, OF NATURE, OF EVERYTHING WE SEE AROUND US.
HARLEY: BY WHO? OH, SORRY, "WHOM?"
MISS T: CARE FOR A DRINK?
HARLEY: DON'T MIND IF I DO

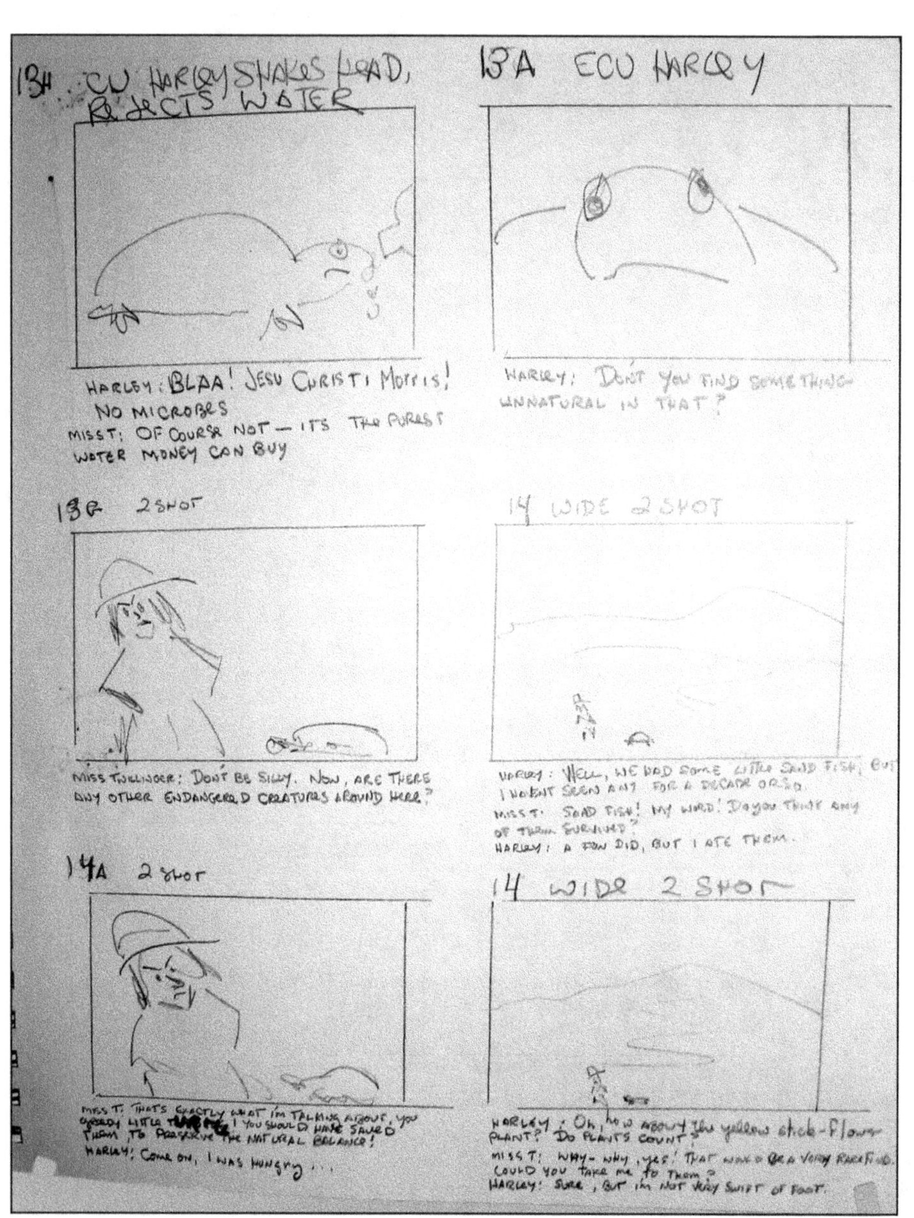

13H   CU HARLEY SHAKES HEAD,
       REJECTS WATER
HARLEY: BLAA! JESU CHRISTI MORRIS!
   NO MICROBES
MISS T: OF COURSE NOT — ITS THE PUREST
WATER MONEY CAN BUY

13A   ECU HARLEY
HARRY: DON'T YOU FIND SOMETHING
UNNATURAL IN THAT?

13B   2 SHOT
MISS TWILLINGER: DON'T BE SILLY. NOW, ARE THERE
ANY OTHER ENDANGERED CREATURES AROUND HERE?

14   WIDE 2 SHOT
HARLEY: WELL, WE HAD SOME LITTLE SAND FISH, BUT
I HAVENT SEEN ANY FOR A DECADE OR SO.
MISS T: SAND FISH! MY WORD! DO YOU THINK ANY
OF THEM SURVIVED?
HARLEY: A FEW DID, BUT I ATE THEM.

14A   2 SHOT
MISS T: THATS EXACTLY WHAT I'M TALKING ABOUT, YOU
GREEDY LITTLE TWERP! YOU SHOULD HAVE SAVED
THEM TO PRESERVE THE NATURAL BALANCE!
HARLEY: COME ON, I WAS HUNGRY . . .

14   WIDE 2 SHOT
HARLEY: OH, HOW ABOUT THE YELLOW STICK-FLOWER
PLANT? DO PLANTS COUNT?
MISS T: WHY— WHY, YES! THAT WOULD BE A VERY RARE FIND.
COULD YOU TAKE ME TO THEM?
HARLEY: SURE, BUT I'M NOT VERY SWIFT OF FOOT.

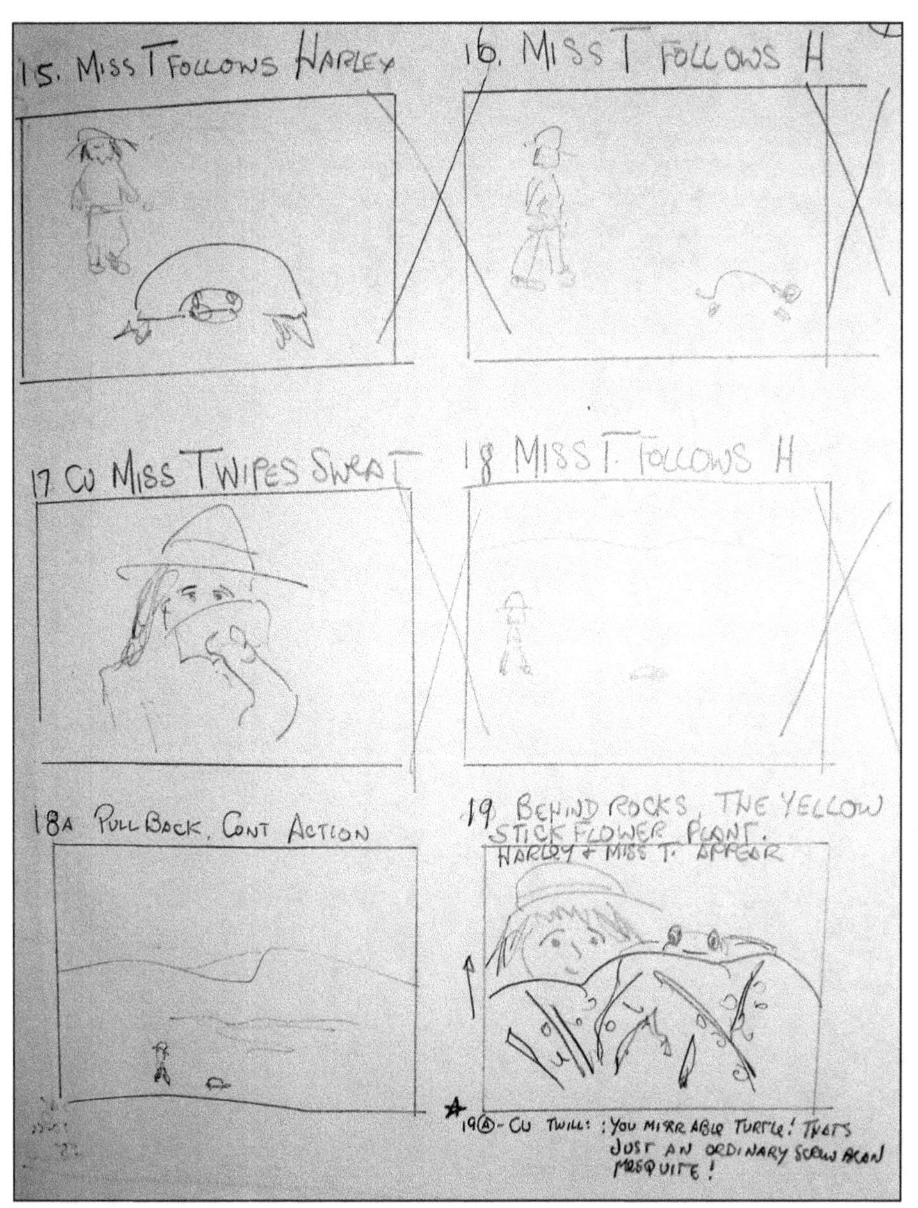

15. MISS T FOLLOWS HARLEY
16. MISS T FOLLOWS H
17 CU MISS T WIPES SWEAT
18 MISS T. FOLLOWS H
18A PULL BACK, CONT ACTION
19. BEHIND ROCKS, THE YELLOW
STICK FLOWER PLANT.
HARLEY & MISS T. APPEAR
19(A) - CU TWILL: YOU MISERABLE TURTLE! THATS
JUST AN ORDINARY SCREW BEAN
MESQUITE!

*19B, C, D HARLEY/TWILL DIALOGUE

20 HARLEY + THE PLANT   21. MISS T.'S ALARM

23. SIDE ANGLE, MISS T.
FALLS BEHIND BOULDER

24 CU. MISS T. IN AGONY

MISS T; OHH, MY GOD!

24A PULL BACK TO REVEAL MISS T. WITH
HER LEG BENT & CAUGHT BETWEEN
TWO BOULDERS.

MISS TWILLINGER: MY GOD, MY GOD,
THE PAIN! HELP ME!

24B PULL BACK TO SHOW HARLEY WATCHING

MISS TWILLINGER: I'M STUCK! I CAN'T
GET OUT OF HERE! SAY SOMETHING!
DO SOMETHING! OH, MY GOD, MY GOD,
MY GOD!

24C CU MISS TWILLINGER
SEES HARLEY IS LEAVING

MISS TWILLINGER: WAIT!

24D HARLEY WALKS OUT OF SHOT

MISS TWILLINGER: STOP! WHERE
ARE YOU GOING?

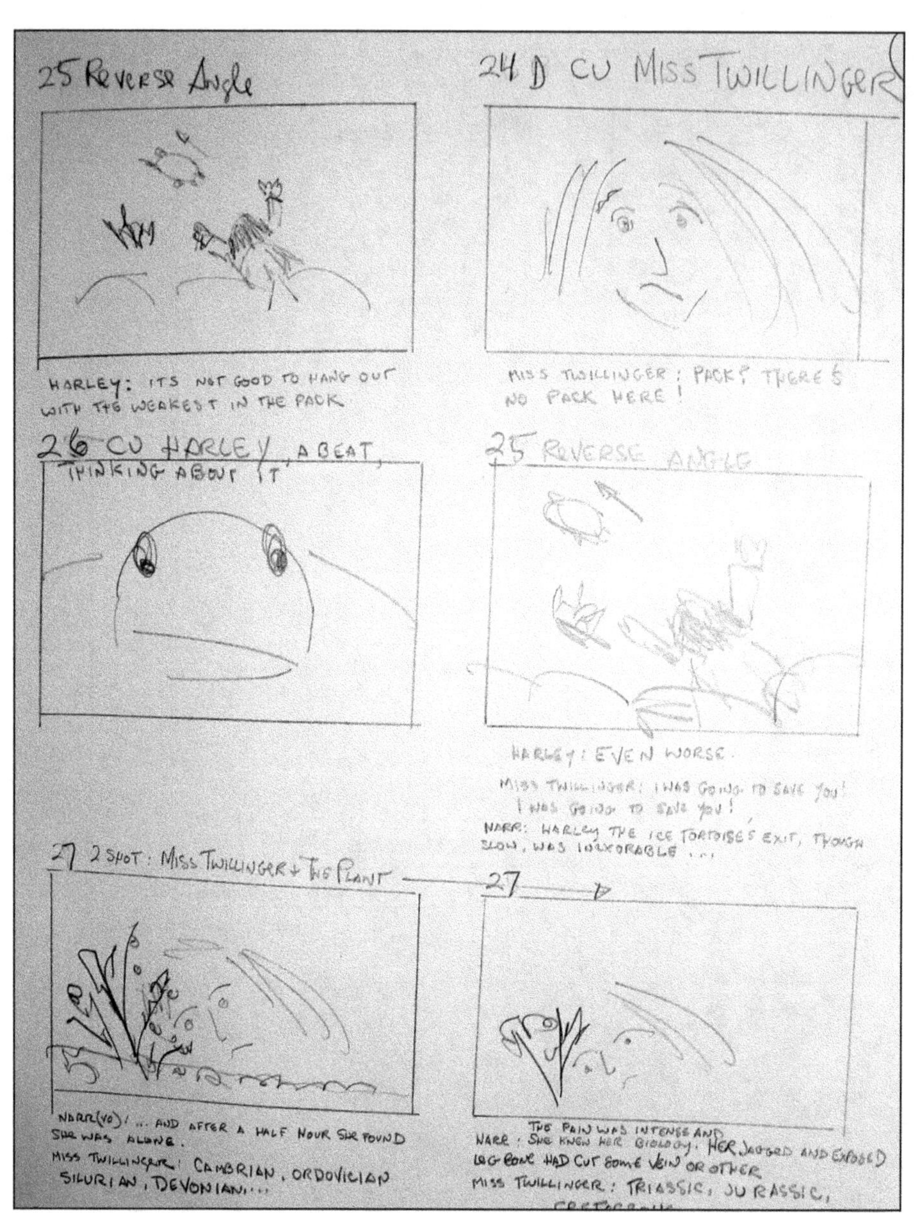

25 Reverse Angle
24 D CU MISS TWILLINGER
HARLEY: ITS NOT GOOD TO HANG OUT WITH THE WEAKEST IN THE PACK
MISS TWILLINGER: PACK? THERE'S NO PACK HERE!
26 CU HARLEY, A BEAT, THINKING ABOUT IT
25 REVERSE ANGLE
HARLEY: EVEN WORSE.
MISS TWILLINGER: I WAS GOING TO SAVE YOU! I WAS GOING TO SAVE YOU!
NARR: HARLEY THE ICE TORTOISE'S EXIT, THOUGH SLOW, WAS INEXORABLE ...
27 2 SHOT: MISS TWILLINGER + THE PLANT
27
NARR (VO): ... AND AFTER A HALF HOUR SHE FOUND SHE WAS ALONE.
MISS TWILLINGER: CAMBRIAN, ORDOVICIAN, SILURIAN, DEVONIAN...
NARR: THE PAIN WAS INTENSE AND SHE KNEW HER BIOLOGY. HER JAGGED AND EXPOSED LEG BONE HAD CUT SOME VEIN OR OTHER
MISS TWILLINGER: TRIASSIC, JURASSIC, CRETACEOUS

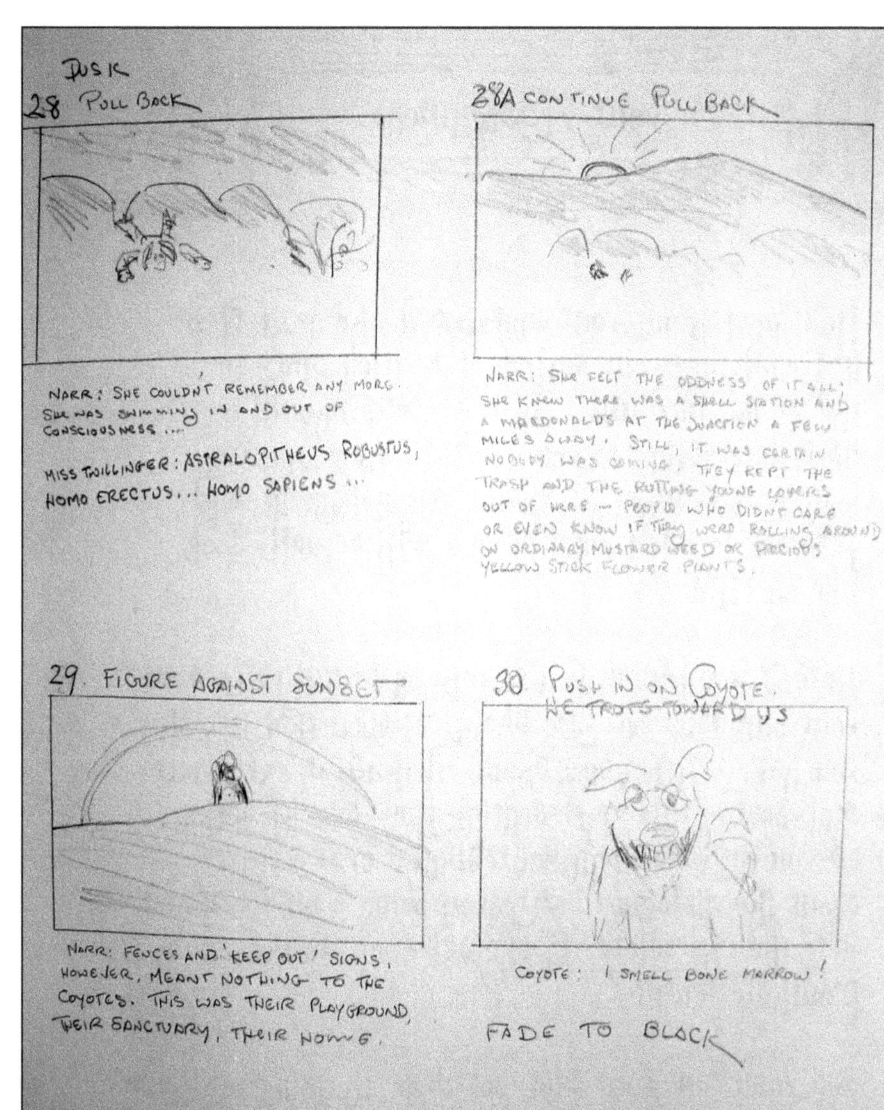

NARR: SHE COULDN'T REMEMBER ANY MORE. SHE WAS SWIMMING IN AND OUT OF CONSCIOUSNESS ...

MISS TWILLINGER: ASTRALOPITHEUS ROBUSTUS, HOMO ERECTUS... HOMO SAPIENS ...

NARR: SHE FELT THE ODDNESS OF IT ALL; SHE KNEW THERE WAS A SHELL STATION AND A MACDONALD'S AT THE JUNCTION A FEW MILES AWAY. STILL, IT WAS CERTAIN NOBODY WAS COMING. THEY KEPT THE TRASH AND THE RUTTING YOUNG LOVERS OUT OF HERE — PEOPLE WHO DIDN'T CARE OR EVEN KNOW IF THEY WERE ROLLING AROUND ON ORDINARY MUSTARD SEED OR PRECIOUS YELLOW STICK FLOWER PLANTS.

NARR: FENCES AND 'KEEP OUT' SIGNS, HOWEVER, MEANT NOTHING TO THE COYOTES. THIS WAS THEIR PLAYGROUND, THEIR SANCTUARY, THEIR HOME.

COYOTE: I SMELL BONE MARROW!

FADE TO BLACK

Now sketch out your storyboard, the next step in translating your outline or written story to the visual medium. This process should be most interesting to you: at this stage you can look back to what was your original intent, and forward to what your scenes will actually look like on film.

Here I would ask you to rely on humility to save your butt later on. Be skeptical about that which you have written and sketched thusfar. Is your storyboard truly representing the flow of action as you envision it in your mind's eye? How about the dialogue? Are you being a bit too wordy? Are the characters "in character" or are they simply mouthing words?

As you draw your storyboard, be thinking of these things: Character. Action. Dialogue.

9 - EVALUATE

As you work smartly to turn your idea, outline or short story into a visual presentation, you are again confronted with the immutable considerations of **Time, Money & Talent.** Looking at your storyboard, you may find complications you had not considered before. Do you know how to stage a fight scene? Have you figured in the production difficulties (costs) of filming a high speed chase? Can you find actors capable of acting out your story? If you can find them, can you afford them? Is there a cheaper way to do things that will put similar production values on the screen for less money?

I

TALKING ABOUT LESS EXPENSIVE WAYS TO PUT INTEREST UP ON THE SCREEN, THIS SCENE FROM A BOOK VIDEO FOR THE POPULAR TWISTED TAILS ANTHOLOGIES RELIES ON SEVERAL TRICKS TO KEEP VIEWER ATTENTION. POPPING THE BOOKS ON SCREEN ONE AT A TIME HELPS RIVET THE VIEWERS EYE TO THE MESSAGE. AND DERON DOUGLAS' BRILLIANT COVER ARTWORK DOESN'T HURT, EITHER. STILL, ATTRACTIVE AS THIS FRAME IS, AND EVEN THOUGH THE VO NARR ALSO STATES THE PITCH LINE ABOUT J. RICHARD JACOBS, FRAMES LIKE THIS CAN HARDLY COMPETE WITH ANIMATION, WITH MODERN ADVANCED ELECTRONIC SPECIAL EFFECTS OR WITH WELL DONE LIVE ACTION. [SEE THIS VIDEO AT http://www.youtube.com/watch?v=VhwjhU3E5Tw]

THE MINIMALIST LOW BUDGET SITUATION

You personally will *write, produce, direct and perform many other tasks you can't even begin to imagine until you get into it. You will be half crazy for the duration of the shoot. Your wife may be gone when you are finished and your kids will not remember your name.*

You can shoot stills, and buy some inexpensive stock stills. *In post production you can do limited 'camera moves' on photos.*

You can probably devise *an in-home sound studio for under $1,000. If you don't have this money or a geek friend with gear, you will be limited to music or to silence, and to on-screen art cards.*

You can't afford complicated live action

With careful planning, you can buy *stock music, stock special effects and maybe some stock live action footage.*

Using PhotoShop or other software, you can generate *art cards and superimpose sentences to tell your story. Remember, pacing is limited to the average number of seconds it takes the average person to read anything. Increase your odds by using clear typefaces and as few words as possible.*

With inexpensive editing software *like Cyberlink Power Director, you will be able to add life to your images with moves on the stills, and add music and some dissolves, fades, and other effects.*

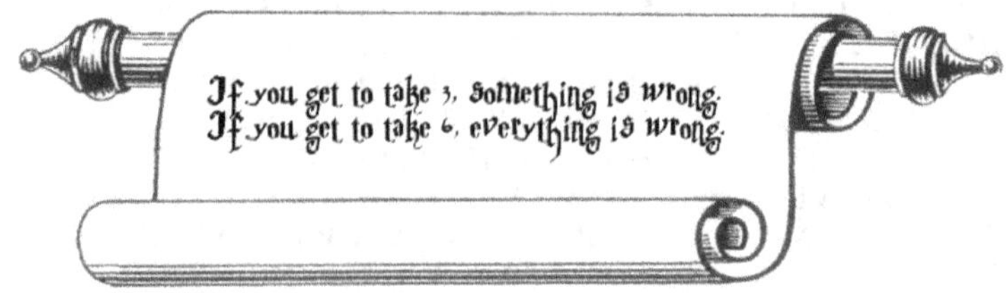

A FEW *"SUPER-LOW"* LOW BUDGET TECHNIQUES

Small live action cast *of one to three people.*

A bare-bones crew: *A cameraman and one assistant jack-of-all-trades*

Beg, borrow or rent *the best camera you can lay your hands on. It must have in camera sound, auto focus and a good tripod.*

You will shoot *indoors (if possible)*

You will use *no fancy camera moves.*

If you need to truck or pan *you can beg, or borrow a wheelchair.*

You will work quickly and quietly *to get in, shoot and get out of locations as you have no money for fees and no time to talk about it.*

Aim for a one or two day shoot. *Try to avoid outdoor night scenes.*

> **'REGULAR' LOW BUDGET TECHNIQUES (ADD ON)**
>
> **Count on no more than a** *two to three day shoot and three to four actors.*
> **Crew:** *Cameraman, sound man and boom man, assist cameraman, maybe a lighting man, and a go-fur.*
> **Aim for** *easy, close, free (or cheap) locations.*
> **If possible, avoid** *night shots, animals, sunsets, water shots.*

At this middle stage in the process, 'simple' methods sometimes present themselves as a way out of the conundrum of production circumstances that you may begin to feel are trapping you. It is tempting to use still photographs and a Voice Over Narration (VO NARR) to carry the story, eliminating the need for a sound crew on location. Or, you might think not to use any voice at all, but rather to carry the story line by means of art cards or 'supers', that is, type superimposed over scenes. Another common 'solution' is to use all camera moves on stills. In this sort of production, your storyboard is very important; in a sense, it *totally represents* the look and feel of what your filmic venture will become.

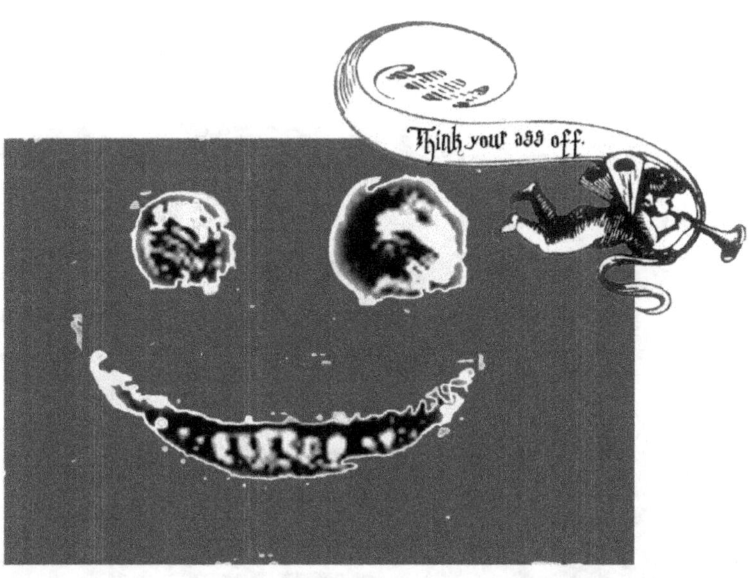

IN THE BOOK TRAILER FOR MY NOVEL "THE HEART OF DESIRE", I NEEDED A VISUAL REPRESENTATION OF THE UNCARING IMMORTALS WHO TINKER WITH THE HERO'S FATE. THIS FLOATING SPECTER PROVIDED THE UNEASY IMAGERY I WAS LOOKING FOR. IT COST ME NOTHING. IF YOU CAN FIGURE OUT EXACTLY WHERE IT CAME FROM AND HOW I CRAFTED IT AND PROVIDE ME WITH YOUR EMAIL ADDRESS, I WILL SEND YOU A PDF FREE COPY OF "THE HEART OF DESIRE". [YOU CAN STUDY THIS BOOK VIDEO AT http://www.youtube.com/watch?v=k1XlR92QiAE]

Extreme low budget techniques, while at times effective, can also narrowly define the nature of the visual presentation, limiting it in predictable ways. A brief study of the modern phenomena of so-called book trailers or book videos (those low cost internet commercials that abound on YouTube and other sites) shows the benefits and restrictions of these methods. In the interest of saving money, one gives up motion, immediacy and interest. Art cards are inexpensive and relatively easy to produce, but they slow down the pace of the story (you've seen'silent' movies), as do supers. Remember, both art cards and supers slow down the pace of the presentation to the estimated speed at which the average viewer is able to read.

HERE IS A PIVOTAL SCENE FROM A BOOK TRAILER PROMOTING "HOLLYWOOD HAVOC", MY *EPIC AUTHORS AWARD* WINNING ACTION THRILLER NOVEL. IN THIS DOCTORED STILL PHOTOGRAPH, I HAVE PHOTOSHOPPED MY HERO, LOW BUDGET MOVIE PRODUCER MATT HAVOC, INTO A CEMENT TRUCK HE THINKS CONTAINS SMUGGLED DIAMONDS. IN POST PRODUCTION, USING CYBERLINK'S POWER DIRECTOR SOFTWARE, I WAS ABLE TO PUSH IN ON THE STILL SHOT TO A CLOSER IMAGE OF MATT GRINNING , NOT REALIZING HE IS DRIVING OFF WITH A NUCLEAR DEVICE IMPORTED INTO THE USA BY TERRORISTS IN AN EFFORT TO BLOW UP LOS ANGELES. [THIS BOOK VIDEO IS AVAILABLE FOR VIEWING AT http://www.youtube.com/watch?v=271mlI-J7jg&feature=related]

Not to say that you couldn't or shouldn't use low budget solutions, but remember the ancient wise saying (from the 1960's) *Every form of refuge has its price.* There are some very well done, attractive and effective book trailers; however, most authors would die for a live actor to deliver a few dramatic lines or a high speed car chase to wow potential viewers. But they can't afford it…me either. When I do trailers for my own books, I use every low budget trick I can think of. For instance, when I wanted to show that Jack Larch, a highly successful Hollywood writer and a player in my romantic suspense novel, "The Freight Train of Love", is a disaster on the streets of Tinseltown, I couldn't show the wreck when he upended his hot girlfriend's Porsche speedster (that she bought from him that he bought from a dealer who said it was 'Steve McQueen's car'). But a friend of mine who is into automotive memorabilia got me a picture of that car and I showed it flipping upside down, along with the narration telling us Jack is notorious as one of the worst drivers in Los Angeles.

A FRAME FROM THE BOOK TRAILER FOR MY NOVEL "THE FREIGHT TRAIN OF LOVE". BOOK TRAILERS ARE INSTRUCTIONAL IN THAT THEY SHOW YOU HOW MUCH YOU CAN PUT ON THE SCREEN FOR VERY LITTLE PRODUCTION MONEY. HOWEVER, THESE SHOOTS DO DEMAND CONSIDERABLE PREPRODUCTION AND POST PRODUCTION EFFORT. THE SHOT OF STEVE MCQUEEN'S UPSIDE DOWN PORSCHE, COURTESY OF MICHAEL KEYSER, AUTOSPORTS MARKETING, LTD. IF YOU DON'T HAVE ANY PHOTOS OR KNOW ANY FRIENDLY STILLS SNAPPERS, THERE ARE SOME VERY GOOD STILLS STOCK LIBRARIES, FEATURING SCENES FROM NATURE TO CASTLES TO TAUT AND TAWNY COUPLES IN STEAMY POSES. AND WITH A LITTLE PLANNING YOU CAN MIX LIVE ACTION SHOTS WITH STILL PHOTOS. [TAKE A LOOK AT THIS LOW BUDGET BOOK TRAILER AT http://www.youtube.com/watch?v=7nW19uAJS2s&feature=related]

So, with the storyboard in hand, it is time to evaluate whether you have the Time, Money and Talent to pull this thing off . If not, what must you change? What *can* you change? Should you just quit and look for some other short story you've written that might work better? Or can you get by with cutting out some actors? Can you change a few locations, shoot in the day rather than at night, shoot indoors where you can control the lighting and not worry about the weather or the natural changes in light as the sun crosses the heavens and begins to sink in the west? Now is the time to evaluate and to plot out the course of your production. Let's take a moment to walk through the production of a very low budget short film. Here's a nice idea about shooting a bear in the woods. Of course, it's no ordinary bear and no ordinary shooter:

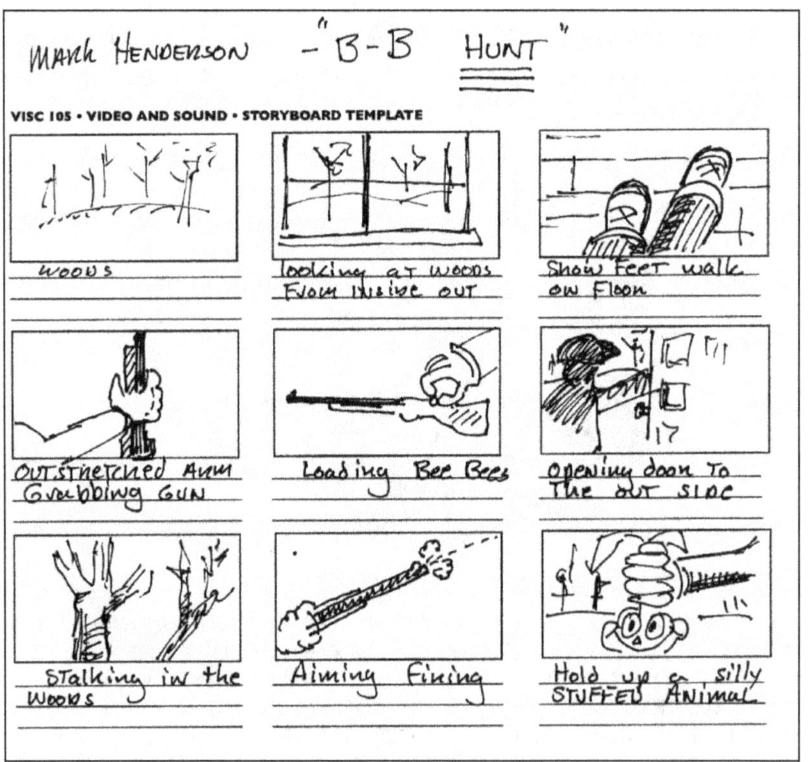

<u>MARK HENDERSON STORYBOARDS</u> HIS"B-B HUNT", A VIDEO HE WANTS TO SHOOT. HIS PROJECT WILL HAVE A WIDE LATITUDE FOR INTERPRETATION, IN THAT IT REPRESENTS AN ORIGINAL IDEA IN HIS MIND, RATHER THAN A SHORT STORY ALREADY WRITTEN. YOU CAN SEE HOW "THE BEAR HUNT TURNED OUT ON YOUTUBE AND COMPARE IT TO HIS ORIGINAL STORYBOARD.

Mark Henderson was resourceful in his production.
He used the woods near his home as the location, so there
were no fees involved, and he didn't have to worry that the
neighbors were going to complain. A closer examination of his
storyboard should tell you that he's keeping a secret—he
doesn't want the viewers to know who the hunter is until he
reveals it. This decision on his part proves to be perhaps the
most difficult aspect of the video that he must direct. He has to
show something of his main character in at least half of the
frames; "Feet walking on the floor", "Outstretched arm grabbing
gun", "Loading B-B's, and so on. It is very difficult to keep this
sort of secret and still show the flow of action. How do you
capture the action without revealing the identity of the
protagonist? Think of it this way: The main character is
attracted to something in the woods. That something is out
there and is deemed (by the main character) to be hunt-able.
The main character resolves to get a gun and go after whatever
is out there. Serious stuff, but in filming, Mark doesn't stick with

131

this objective. And the edge is taken off when, in the scenes as Mark has recorded them we come to realize it is a very young person going after whatever is in the woods. And the B-B's become heart shaped "affection bullets". The story turns out to have a sweet ending, something of fresh allegory for a young child's affection for her stuffed toy.

So Mark ended up enriching and defining his storyboard as he went along, using stop-motion techniques and a wonderful music track (Mark is a highly successful composer and musician). Whether he is a true, died-in-the wool pantser— or only thought to enrich his story as he went along—doesn't matter as much as it would if he was *adapting*. But if you start out with your own short story—or with a money person's idea— you can't always do that.

MARK HENDERSON'S FINISHED VIDEO HAS A RICHNESS AND HUMAN TOUCH NOT DISPLAYED IN HIS STORYBOARD. WRITER DIRECTORS OFTEN HANDLE THEIR STORYBOARDING THIS WAY. SOME DON'T EVEN BOTHER TO SKETCH THEM OUT, RELYING ON THE VISUALIZATIONS THEY HAVE IN THEIR HEAD. AS A GENERAL RULE, THE MORE COMPLEX THE SHOOT (AND THE LESS TIME YOU HAVE FOR YOUR PRODUCTION), THE MORE INCENTIVE YOU WILL HAVE TO SKETCH OUT THE MAJOR ACTIONS AND TRANSITIONS. [TO SEE HOW THIS TURNED OUT FOR MARK HENDERSON GO TO http://tinyurl.com/thebearhunt]

The idea behind filming my short story "Extinction" was to render visually the same concept that I'd written as a short story. Reading my adaptation and looking at the storyboard, you may not suspect the world of hurt and trouble I was about to step into. I could write an article about it, titled *"The Trouble With Turtles"*.

Yes, of course I googled DESERT TORTOISES. And I had one other trick up my sleeve. Some years before, my early filmic mentor, Nelson B. Winkless, jr. had actually lip-synched a tortoise, getting the creature to pitch the benefits of a Motorola color TV set. True, it had been a giant sea turtle, but I didn't figure there would be much difference. Looking back, I would have been wiser to take a trip to the Los Angeles Zoo and spend some time hanging out where they kept the desert creatures. I could have gotten to know the lay of the land, so to speak, maybe even figure out what they ate for lunch and whether they would need a break (like a union turtle might) or if they could go all day without a nap.

ON THE DISNEY LOT, I SHOT FOOTAGE OF SOME ORANGE-AND-BLACK TARANTULAS FOR AN EARLY TEASE TRAILER I MADE FOR THE MOVIE "SOMETHING WICKED THIS WAY COMES". TEASE TRAILERS OFTEN INVOLVE RESOURCEFULNESS, AS THE BEST SPECIAL EFFECTS GENERALLY HAVEN'T BEEN GENERATED, AND YET THE STUDIO NEEDS TO PRODUCE CONVINCINGLY EXCITING COMMERCIALS TO RUN IN MOVIE HOUSES UP TO A YEAR BEFORE THE ACTUAL FILM OPENS.

You will have a fight on your hands, as you, the writer, confronts you, the producer and you, the director. It's a necessary conflict; you don't want to put it off until you're on the set burning money while *the three of you* face an unresolved problem like words that won't fit comfortably in an actor's mouth or a bird that won't fly the right direction in the sky. You are the creator of the world of your movie. Producing it will convince you that to have things run smoothly takes more than miracles. You are conducting a godlike enterprise, but remember—*the devil is in the details.* While glib, the proof of this statement is that, from the moment you decide to develop your story idea into a film or video, you are fighting every step of the way to keep alive the world of your creation as you originally envisioned it.

DO YOU BELIEVE YOU CAN TRUST A CREATURE THAT LOOKS LIKE THIS TO KEEP YOUR PRODUCTION ON SCHEDULE AND ON BUDGET? EVEN A WILY AND EXPERIENCED FELLOW LIKE ME HAD MY HANDS FULL WITH HARLEY, THE SURLY AND SELF-WILLED TORTOISE.

Let's talk about your money. Do you have a lot of it? More to the point, do you have enough to do a good job producing the concept you have selected? You wouldn't want to waste your most excellent writing, that has probably won readership and acclaim (or, some day will)…You wouldn't want your terrific idea misrepresented as a terrible short film simply because you didn't have the money or time to produce it right. Better not to make the attempt. Or, if you are driven to do this, be absolutely certain to select one of your concepts you know you can produce beautifully. And when all that is said and done, *be flexible on the set.* Yes, you will want to stay true to the meaning and intent of your story, but you don't want to lose your house in Beverly Hills or that love nest on Maui just because some creature with a platter on its back won't cooperate.

YOU CAN RENT A PRIVATE JET IF IT IS A PROP YOU ABSOLUTELY MUST HAVE TO MAKE YOUR VIDEO WORK, BUT THEY ARE EXPENSIVE AND YOU HAVE TO BUY AT LEAST A HALF A DAY EVEN IF IT JUST SITS THERE ON THE GROUND. MAYBE YOU COULD STEAL A SHOT AT THE LOCAL AIRPORT?

A few words about your private life. Perhaps you've dedicated an hour or two of every day to your writing (maybe 4 to 6 am when the significant other and the kids are sleeping).

But producing a short film is a different kind of vixen, more shrill and demanding even than that writerly muse you've been working hard to satisfy. If you're going to make this video happen, you have to cunningly arrange to set aside the necessary time. That includes the days for preproduction, location scouting, casting, and gathering your crew and equipment. And the days of shooting. And then the days necessary to convert all that raw footage you've shot into your epic masterpiece, then add the music and special effects, and then get it in front of the public eye.

Is your impossible dream truly impossible? You have to decide, and better now than later, when you are locked into the production, standing on the set torching your money with an actress or a budget—or a turtle—that's too nasty to handle.

Evaluate. Do it now before it's too late!
Is this really still your story, the one you want
to tell? Does it say what you want? And can
you beg, borrow or steal the bucks to do it well?
And...can you schedule the time in your busy life?

10 - SCOUT WELL

"The three most important things are location, location, location!"

--Overheard at every location scouting expo I've ever been to.

IF YOU CAN AFFORD IT, YOU WANT THE PLACE THAT BEST REALIZES YOUR VISION. I LOCATION SCOUTED A HARBOR SCENE TO PROMOTE DISNEY'S MOVIE "SPLASH". I SCOUTED MARINA DEL REY HARBOR THE NIGHT BEFORE AND RENTED A BOAT. IT SEEMED PERFECT, BUT THE DAY OF THE SHOOT, JET AIRPLANES TOOK OFF FROM LAX EVERY MINUTE AND FORTY FIVE SECONDS, JUST WHEN "SPLASH" DIRECTOR RONNIE HOWARD WAS SAYING HIS LINES. AFTER THAT, HE NEVER CALLED ME.

As you progress as a do-it-yourself vidmaker, you will find more and more ways to *game the system*, to put more value on the screen for a lower cost. For instance, if you have convinced yourself to do a historical period piece, you can establish the time period and general location with an easy stills camera move on a vintage postcard or photograph, and that move can be timed in post production with your editing system. Then you can dissolve to live action shots…medium and close shots to carry the story. In the book trailer for my murder mystery novel "Foul", I used mostly stills, but inserted four short live-action shots to punch up the visual interest. [YOU CAN STUDY THE "FOUL" BOOK TRAILER AT http://www.youtube.com/watch?v=-sM-TSA2PrI]

PUSH IN ON PHOTO TO THE LADY WITH THE BROOM. CROSS DISS TO LIVE ACTION, THE LADY FURIOUSLY SWEEPING IN HER KITCHEN. OR, PUSH IN TO FEATURE THE MAN AND HORSES. DISS TO THE MAN, PLOWING HIS FIELDS...

You can maintain your period feel at a lower cost by intro-ing a scene with an old photo and then pinching your live action scenes so that the action plays in a narrower field of view, for instance one poker table or maybe an old time piano player instead of the entire barroom interior. You can make a tighter scene play with good use of props. A glimpse of whiskey bottles, mirrors and a painting of dancing ladies on the wall behind the bar, for instance.

PUSH IN TO LIVE ACTION IN EITHER BAR. IN THE IRISH MEN ONLY BAR, THE MEN ARE DOING A DRUNKEN JIG. IN THE "FAMILY" GERMAN SALOON NEXT DOOR, MEN AND THEIR WIVES ARE DINING WHILE A SMALL UMPAH BAND PLAYS ON A RAISED DIAZ. BUT YOU DON'T NEED MUSICIANS OR A BAND, AS THE MUSIC CAN CARRY THE SCENE, EVEN IF YOU TIGHTEN IT DOWN TO TWO OR FOUR MEN OR ONE FAMILY AT A TABLE.

For some films, the illusion of a location is enough to carry the scene. If you are going to shoot in a bar, a restaurant, a whore house or entirely inside a car (four locations that are favored by many short films destined for film festivals or the internet), scouting the location is not as important as it might be if you wanted to shoot in a Columbian jungle or on a windswept Irish beach. But if you do need city slums, a beach or the interior of a grocery store, you've got to figure all that out beforehand. Filming urban decay can be difficult and even dangerous, and while you may be able to steal a simple beach shot (many recreation and vacation locations demand permits), you are going to have to film in a grocery story at night, when it is closed to normal business. If you are going to film in a cemetery, you don't want to make a big deal out if it, and you don't have to…sometimes a stills shot is all you need.

Check the two photos below (the larger one of the fireman and the inset of him at his regular job). There are occasions in low budget filmmaking, when these can be enough to establish the story in terms of location and time period. But once you begin, you have to stay true to the look and feel of what you have introduced, even as you pinch down the shots because you need to economize and you can't find a period firehouse or a century old piano making factory. You may locate a local museum that has an old hand-pumper fire wagon, or a wood working or pattern-maker wood shop that can double for the factory.

The point is, as you're thinking things through, you have to evaluate what you have visualized, written in your script and storyboarded. Just what does EXT. SUNSET ON THE MOJAVE DESERT means in terms of Time, Money, and Talent? You have to look for locations that are right for your look, and are also easy to get to and have electricity if you need it. Also, it would be nice to have adequate parking and even rest room facilities (be still my heart). You'll want to quietly inquire if you can get permission to shoot there, or at least be assured you can get the shots you need and beat a hasty retreat before some rancher or gold prospector shows up with a shotgun and starts blowing holes in your production vehicles.

I WENT ON THE INTERNET **TO FIGURE THE EXACT TIME OF SUNSET. UNFORTUNATELY, I HADN'T CALCULATED THAT THE SUN WOULD SET BEHIND A BIG SANDSTONE BLUFF TO THE WEST OF WHERE WE HAD TO SHOOT THE CRITICAL FINAL SCENES. WE LOST FIFTEEN PRECIOUS MINUTES OF DIRECT SUNLIGHT, AND IN THE SCENES WHERE OUR *PROTAGONISTA* FALLS TO THE GROUND I HAD NO TIME TO PICK UP COVERAGE FOR THE DRAMATIC IMPACT THE SCENE DEMANDED. AND IN THE FOLLOWING SCENES, AS OUR ACTRESS WAS LYING ON THE GROUND, THE DREADED EVENING WIND CAME UP AND BLEW SAND AND GRIT IN HER FACE.**

Some matters you can control, and some are out of your scope. For instance, deserts are by nature hot and dry. The minute the sun goes down, a wind comes up that can blow dust in the actors' faces. It was vitally important for me on the "Extinction" shoot to know that in the Spring months the temperature wouldn't be as hot as it gets in August and September. The decision to film in April proved critical, as any later in the year and the desert tortoises would not have been able to do their work. As it was, they could only act in direct sunlight for 45 seconds, after which they needed a rest break of from 15 minutes to an hour. *Lucky we rented three of the obdurate creatures, right?*

<u>MATT KLAWITTER</u> (SHOWN HERE WITH GEO, ONE OF OUR CAMERAMEN) SCOUTED AND FINALLY FOUND THE OVERALL PERFECT LOCATION FOR OUR DRAMATIC SHORT FILM "EXTINCTION".

If your idea calls for a "Chicago urban setting" and you live in Los Angeles, this can be a terrible problem. But you will notice in many television series, and even movies, the exact city isn't as important as keeping the look uniform once you begin filming. So if you want to shoot on Maui in the Sandwich Isles, write that location into your script and find a way to make that happen, perhaps with stills or a stock footage establish shot. Once upon a time not so long ago, movies and television shows were all shot on studio lots. They ended up with a stale feeling of sameness. You will not be troubled with that difficulty.

As a do-it-yourself vidmaker, you may learn some of the art of hit-and-run shot piracy from my Hollywood Havoc novels. In those stories, based on my own sorry real life experiences, young low budget film producer Matt Havoc ducks and dodges irate citizens and alert policemen in his efforts to produce low budget *schlock* pulpers for his boss, Vinnie Berger of Berger

Royal Productions. It's hard to hold focus and *get it in the can*, as they say, when housewives are shrieking and bouncers are coming at you with baseball bats and gang members are waving beer bottles and swinging bicycle chains. *Welcome to my world, brave young vidmakers!*

BARELY AN HOUR AND A HALF NORTH OF LOS ANGELES AND 15 MINUTES NORTH OF LODGING IN THE TOWN OF MOJAVE, RED ROCK CANYON FEATURED THE RUGGED DESERT LANDSCAPE WE NEEDED FOR "EXTINCTION"

Not paying enough attention to your locations can kill your project. Even if your scenes are all simple and easy as somebody's garage, somebody's back yard, somebody's basement, and so on, you have to be aware that getting from one location to the next will cost you time. And, equally as important, the look and feel of the place has to be right for your story.

JUST BECAUSE IT IS A _CABIN_ DOESN'T MEAN IT WORKS AS A RUN DOWN OLD FUR TRAPPER'S CABIN. STILL, SOMETIMES BY MOVING IN CLOSE YOU CAN SHOOT A SMALL PIECE OF THE CABIN AND IT WILL WORK.

Be nimble about getting your shots. If you decide not to pay money for locations, you have to know how to set up and break down your equipment quickly.

A FEW WORDS TO THE WISE:

You are not actually _stealing footage._ You are _borrowing a location._

Urban businesses often feel they own their street front 'looks', and the local city laws may be in their favor. Sometimes you can convince them to shoot for free because of the 'good publicity'.

Local police may not like you. Be prepared to strike set and move on swiftly and quietly like a thief in the night.

Guard your camera and lighting equipment at all times.

Be unswervingly, unfailingly polite, and **always** clean up after your shoot, that is, unless folks are after you with impressive firepower.

Re-read your screenplay and study your storyboard
with an eye to the practicality of your venture.
Just where will you be shooting? How can you
gain access to the locations you want and need?

If you have written the impossible into your script,
now is the time to change it.

Think ahead to what it will be like at those locations
the moment you start rolling your vid camera. If you
are filming indoors, will the electrical system have
enough amps so you can draw power without blowing
fuses or breakers every 30 seconds? And, if you are
filming outdoors, if it's a night shot, will you need
portable power packs to handle hit-and-run style
lighting?

What about noise? Crowd control? Pesky curiosity
seekers? Road traffic? Police interference?

11 – BREAKDOWN

"How much is this going to cost me per minute?"
*--Famous Indy Television Producer, after yawning
through a pitch for one of my creative ideas.*

How long is a shot? Not how long it will take you to
shoot it, but how long (in seconds) is any shot in your script? In
my short video, how long does it take Harley to say "It's not
good to hang out with the weakest in the pack."? Miss
Twillinger reacts, saying, "Pack? There's no *pack* here!" How
long does it take her to say that? You might say Harley's line
would take six seconds, and you'd be pretty close. The length
of each shot is important, because when you add them all up,
they tell you how long your film will be. You'll want to know
whether your finished masterpiece will be five, ten or fifteen
minutes long. So the first thing you should do in your breakdown
is go through the movie script and time each scene with a
stopwatch as best you can.

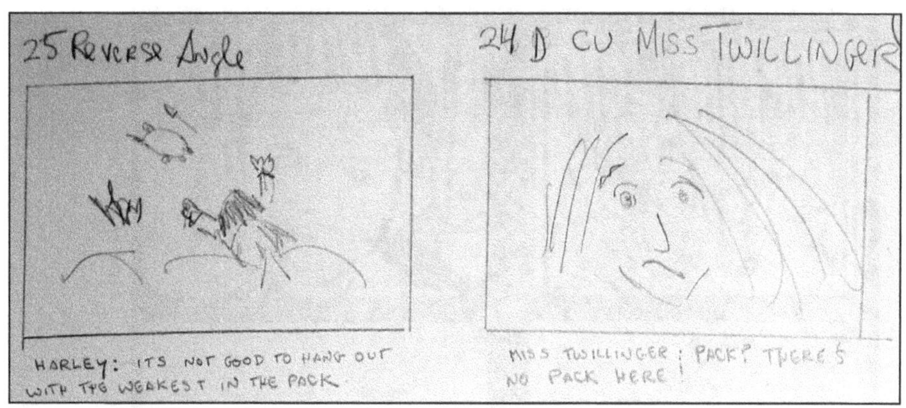

**I THOUGHT I KNEW TORTOISES. I GUESS IT WAS A CASE OF *SEEN ONE
TURTLE, YOU'VE SEEN THEM ALL.* WHILE MISS TWILLINGER'S LINE
WORKED WELL, HARLEY'S ABSOLUTELY DID NOT. INSTEAD OF A CLOSE
UP OF HARLEY SAYING HIS LINE, I HAD TO LAY IT IN OVER HIS
RETREATING BACK. HE PROVED TO BE A DIFFICULT MOVIE STAR IN MANY
WAYS. LUCKY FOR ME I FOUND SOLUTIONS FOR MOST OF MY *TORTOISE
TROUBLES* AS THEY CAME UP, BUT YOU DON'T WANT TOO MANY
SURPRISES WHILE YOU'RE BURNING MONEY ON THE SET.**

Timing your scenes is not as hard as you may think.
Use a stopwatch, and where there's dialogue or narration, say it out loud. You can write the times on each frame in your storyboard, or do a running tab on a notepad, and then add them up later. I began my career as an advertising agency copywriter, writing mostly television commercials. My earliest work was on Kellogg's cereals and Nestlés chocolate bars. When you work in television or radio advertising, timing your work becomes second nature. If it's a 30 second spot, you have to do it in exactly that time without the message seeming forced, rushed or confused. But you don't have to know how to do commercials to time your own video…you just have to remember that you are telling a story, scene by scene. You can set it up with a Voice Over Narrator if you want to, or you can let the story play out through your action and dialogue. However you set it up, use a stopwatch and read each scene out loud or play the action in your mind.

THESE ARE TWO OPENING FRAMES FROM AN EXPERIMENTAL TELEVISION CAMPAIGN I DID FOR KELLOGG'S. OLD LEO BURNETT, THEN RELUCTANTLY NEARING RETIREMENT, WAS INTENSELY INTERESTED IN 'DO-IT-YOURSELF' PRODUCTION AND ENVISIONED THE DAY WHEN ELECTRONIC MEDIA WOULD BLOSSOM AS IT HAS.

When you time the scenes in your short film, your count for the whole film may be off by a minute or two. But if you don't time them, you could be off far more, even by as much as 50 or 60 percent! The step of timing each storyboard frame is not to give you an *exact* run time for the entire presentation, but rather *a reasonable estimate* that you can use as you firm up your visualization. As you already suspect, there will be changes along the way. Pacing will be very important; with dialogue, scenes are subject to delivery, to characterization and the director and actor's interpretations. With mood or scenery shots, you will have some latitude as to length of screen time they might take. If you go back and take a look at scenes #1 and #1a in my storyboard for "Extinction", you'll see they are meant to establish the harsh beauty of the desert, as well as present a 'something' on the two-lane blacktop. Well, in the finished film, those scenes are nearly a half minute in length because I felt we needed that much time to bring across a feeling of the quiet danger that lurks in the natural order of things away from civilization. And I never did establish a 'something' on the road. Action scenes, on the other hand, take very little time at all.

THE BIKER ROARS PAST IN A FEW SECONDS. (THIS IS A RUBBER, FULL SCALE TURTLE MODEL.) NO ANIMALS WERE HARMED ON THIS SHOOT, THOUGH I CAN'T COMPLETELY VERIFY AS TO DESERT ANTS. HAVING BEEN BITTEN IN A BAD PLACE BY DESERT RED ANTS, I HAVE LITTLE COMPASSION AND ZERO EMPATHY FOR THE NASTY CREATURES.

Now that you have estimated as best you can how many seconds of screen time each shot will take, you must calculate how much time out of your shoot day you need to successfully capture each shot. How many takes will you need? What are the complications?

Working backwards from the individual scenes, you then determine the number of days needed to shoot the entire story. You also have to map out the number of indoor and outdoor shots, and the day or night shots, and those you might want to shot at sunrise or sunset. You know you can't control the weather, and time will march on whether your actress needs a spot of makeup or not.

IN THIS EXPERIMENTAL COMMERCIAL THE STORY IS WILLIE KELLOGG DREAMED OF GOING TO SEA, SO HE BUILT A RAFT AND THEN GOT IN TROUBLE WITH HIS MOM WHEN HE TOOK A BED SHEET FROM HER CLOTHES LINE TO USE FOR A SAIL. LONG STORY SHORT (IT'S A COMMERCIAL, REMEMBER), HE CHANGES HIS MIND AND DECIDES TO FOUND A GREAT BREAKFAST CEREAL COMPANY, INSTEAD. SIMPLE ENOUGH, BUT BUILDING THE RAFT WAS HARDER THAN WE THOUGHT. IT LOOKED OKAY, BUT WHEN WE LAUNCHED IT, IT BARELY FLOATED, AND WHEN OUR YOUNG ACTOR SCRAMBLED ON BOARD, IT TIPPED AND TILTED, SLIDING THE YOUTH AND HIS ANGRY CAT INTO THE POND. WE ENDED UP PROPPING THE RAFT FROM UNDERNEATH IN SHALLOW WATER AND BARELY GOT THE SHOT BEFORE IT CAME APART.

Just how many shoot days will you need to get your story 'in the can'? When you're watching somebody else shoot a picture, the on-set adventures can be interesting and even amusing. But when it's *your* production, the process can feel like a cruel somebody is burning your hundred dollar bills with a blowtorch. That's why it is important, to the best of your ability, to determine beforehand how long it will take you to shoot each frame that you've drawn on your storyboard. Let's say you've got a shot of somebody walking through the desert. Chances are, this isn't going to be a very difficult shot to capture. But if you've got a person with a desert tortoise walking alongside, it will probably take longer

"BRONCO" BRADLEY MERVILLE TESTS A RUBBER TURTLE RIG BY A ROADSIDE IN THE MOJAVE DESERT WHILE PRODUCER MATT KLAWITTER LOOKS ON. THE RUBBER TURTLE, MOUNTED ON ROLLERS, IS PULLED BY A THIN FISHING LINE. THE RIG PERFORMED VERY WELL WHEN TESTED ON CEMENT IN MY GARAGE, BUT MOVEMENT WAS TOO JERKY AND UNNATURAL ON THE ROUGHER ASPHALT SURFACE OF THE DESERT ROAD. YOU CAN SEE HOW WE WORKED AROUND THE PROBLEM BY VIEWING THE FINISHED "EXTINCTION" VIDEO. [http://preview.tinyurl.com/tort-twil]

Do-it-yourself low budget production is a bit like ice skating—you just have to keep sticking one foot in front of the other to keep from falling on your face. Because you have absolutely no time or money to waste, it helps to pre-plan every detail, as much as is possible. And yet once you roll the dice and your shoot day arrives, you'll find that no matter how hard you tried to pin everything down, reality will squirt out between your fingers and you'll be scrambling to get all your shots in before the sun sets, the rain moves in or the power fails.

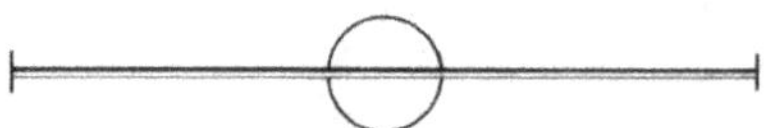

Now break down your storyboard two ways:

First, time your best guestimate of how much time each shot will run in the final cut. Scribble this timing in blue ink on your actual storyboard. (I also use red colored markers with a lot of arrows to indicate camera moves, but some directors prefer to defer this sort of thinking until they are on the set.)

Second, calculate to the best of your ability the amount of time it will take you and your crew to set up, shoot, strike down the set, clean up, and move on to set up for the next shot. Once you have done this, study all the times and figure out how many production days (and nights) you will need to shoot your vid.

12 - CAST IT

**"Want to witness an unfortunate side of human behavior?
Come to an audition. You'll see why they got the name *cattle call.*"**
*--Famous studio casting director who threatens to sue if I
mention her name.*

I NEEDED A BAD BIKER FOR "EXTINCTION", BUT WE COULDN'T FIND ANY
NICE OR PLEASANT HELL'S ANGELS. HOWEVER WE DID COME UP WITH
VERNON IGNATZIO, KNOWN LOCALLY AS "THE WATER GOD' BECAUSE HE
RUNS A WATER PURIFYING SERVICE CALLED WIALANI, BUT HE IS ALSO A
ROUGH-AND-TUMBLE LOOKING BIKER, A NATIVE HAWAIIAN WITH
ANCIENT NATIVE TATTOO DESIGNS ALL OVER HIS ARMS AND LEGS. WHEN
THE DEMIGODS OF PRODUCTION GIVE YOU LEMONS, YOU MAKE
LEMONADE.

**If you don't live in Los Angeles, New York City, or
any other major urban area** you have to be clever to find good
actors who are right for your vid. And if you do live in a big city,
you have to be twice as enterprising because hiring Screen
Actor's Guild members can crush your budget, and not hiring
them can call out the union alarmists.

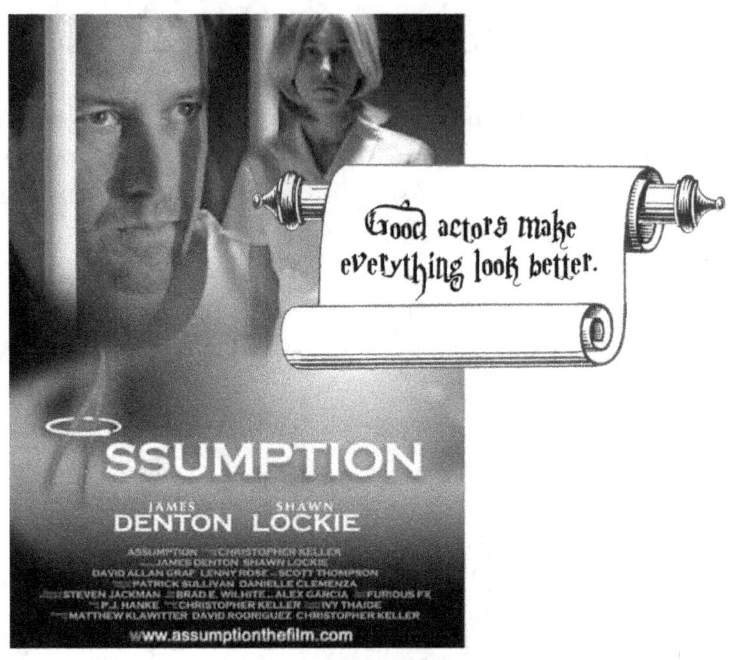

<u>THERE IS ALWAYS A WAY:</u> "ASSUMPTION", WRITTEN AND PRODUCED BY CHRIS KELLER AND PRODUCED BY MATTHEW KLAWITTER, MANAGED TO STAR JAMES DENTON AND SHAWN LOCKIE. FOR MY OWN SHORT FILM "EXTINCTION", I WAS LUCKY THAT MATTHEW'S WIFE IS A FINE ACTRESS AND WAS WILLING TO DO THE PART. IF YOU LIVE IN A PLACE WITH FEWER ACTING RESOURCES, YOU MUST BE MORE RESOURCEFUL. HOWEVER, NEVER DOUBT FOR A SECOND THAT IT CAN BE DONE OR THAT YOU CAN DO IT.

When I started out to make short films and vids, I did not understand actors or acting. I think this was at least in part due to my strict Christian upbringing. I truly believed actors were gypsies who stole an exciting living rather than working for honest wages. My directorial mentor, Arthur Pierson, who himself had worked for Cecil B. DeMille, converted me when he explained how hard Marilyn Monroe had studied to perfect the way she looked and sounded on the screen. Marilyn, he said, would sit patiently in the lobby for hours, hoping some other young actor or actress wouldn't show up for the classes Universal Studios provided their young contract players. Classes in singing, dancing, voice and dramatics that later allowed her to shine with a *natural sexy innocence.* Who knew it took such dogged persistence to appear fresh and naïve?

EARLY ON, I REALIZED THAT IT WOULD HELP TO GET SOME FIRST HAND ACTING EXPERIENCE. HERE I AM IN A BEER SPOT. THE IDEA IS THAT SINCE I AM DRINKING THIS FAMILIAR BRAND BEER (SCHLITZ), I AM NOW POPULAR. NOTICE HOW THE ACTOR ON THE LEFT MISINTERPRETS THE IDEA, USING A SIMPLE PRETZEL TO 'STEAL THE SCENE' FROM ME AND BECOME THE CENTER OF ATTENTION. THIS WAS MY INTRODUCTION TO THE UNREMITTING BATTLES THAT GO ON BETWEEN ACTORS. AND THIS IS WHY, WHEN A STAR PROVES GENEROUS TO HIS FELLOWS AND TO THE DIRECTOR, IT IS WORTHY OF NOTE.

Actors, of course, must know their lines, and should hash out their misunderstandings and refinements beforehand. But on the low end of the production business, the most difficult chore can be finding any actors at all who want to play the part—and can do it with any degree of success. The less suitable they are, the more weight will be placed back on you, the director, so think twice before casting your money man's girlfriend in the lead.

As **a do-it-yourself filmmaker, you will probably be directing.** As director, you must always insist your talent read for their parts. If they can't do the part, no problem, you can find somebody else. But if they are unsuitable for the role and you sign them on anyway, it's your funeral.

The problem with talent is, it is often unavailable when and where you want it, or at an acceptable price. Pay them too much and you'll sink your budgetary ship; too little and you'll have a pouty mess on your hands, trouble on the set. In producing short films with low budgets, it is often a good idea to join a club of young filmmakers. There you may find ambitious actors and actresses available at a reasonable price. I know this seems like a cheap and shoddy way to approach your production, but every vidmaker faces the same difficulties. Actors cost bundles of cash, and if you don't have it, you have to find a way around the problem.

<u>COMMERCIAL AND DOCUMENTARY DIRECTORS</u> LEARN DIFFERENT DISCIPLINES THAN THOSE WHO DEVELOP THEIR ABILITY TO DIRECT DRAMATIC SCENES. MY ADVANCED LESSONS IN DIRECTING *DRAMA* BEGAN WITH SCENES I WROTE BASED ON MY VIETNAM NOVELS AND MY SHORT STORIES ABOUT MY OWN WAR EXPERIENCES. IN THE HEART OF LOS ANGELES, DIRECTING SCENES FOR A MASTERS DIRECTORIAL CLASS I WAS TAKING AT THE DIRECTORS GUILD, I WAS ABLE TO CONVINCE SAG ACTORS TO WORK FOR FREE…FOR THE EXPERIENCE OF WORKING WITH ME AT THE GUILD

Actors can't help themselves; they want to get in front of that camera. This is well to your advantage and may be the only card you can play as a low budget filmmaker. You can give them the opportunity to practice their craft. The danger here is that, if you're paying them very little or not paying them at all, they may be headstrong in their interpretation of their role.

If they want the part, sometimes it seems actors and actresses will do anything to get it. But then, you're stuck with them. Make sure they read for the role. Burn a chip and study the playback before you choose. You might be surprised.

You, as the producer and director, can always fire an actor, but I've never been able to handle this without a great deal of hostility and grief. That's why reading for the part beforehand is critical. Sleep on the takes, review them in the morning, when the talent is taking a shower or at a cattle call somewhere else. Better not to hire them in the first place than to have to dump them in front of the rest of the cast and crew.

If you hire an untested but amateur actor or actress that you prematurely judged had sufficient talent, and things prove otherwise, that could involve dozens of re-takes to get every shot the way you want it, and *that* would easily cost you days on location and suck big money from your budget.

Actors have a million ways to upstage each other and steal audience attention. It is a minor and harmless game until the mischief strays from the intent of your scene. On the other hand, if your thespians are not well enough motivated, they might not show up at all, and I or your Aunt Gladys may not be a decent last minute stand-in.

WHEN CASTING CALLS ARE HELD FOR "PARTY GOERS", "PARTY ANIMALS", "FUN TIME PEOPLE" OR EVEN PICNIC CHURCH GATHERINGS, IT IS COMMON THAT AT LEAST ONE MIME WILL SHOW UP. THEY ARE NEVER HIRED, AND NO ONE KNOWS WHY THIS PHENOMENON OCCURS. DO NOT BE TEMPTED TO GIVE THEM A PART UNLESS YOUR STORY ABSOLUTELY NEEDS A MIME, AS YOUR LIFE ON THE SET WILL BECOME TEDIOUS.

Do not attempt to shoot footage without first
holding casting calls where you have the players
actually read lines for the part they are seeking.
If characterization is the key to the success of
your vid, then it is not improper to ask the two
or three most suitable players back for a second
or even third reading before you make up your
mind as to the very best choice.

Hold your readings in a room or outdoor place
where there are few interruptions as possible.
If the shoot will be outdoors, consider holding
the talent call outdoors, as well.

In the first call, you will read the other lines
to help the actor or actress seeking any part.
In the second or third call, have the players
interact together so you can get an idea of relative
strengths and the mix or blend of the characters.

13 - ABOVE THE LINE

"To get a picture made, we spend millions above-the-line. To get it made right, we spend hundreds of thousands below-the-line."

--Arthur Pierson, long time Hollywood director.

<u>1970 – LEMANS, FRANCE</u>. NIKITA KNATZ (ON THE RIGHT, ON THE STEPS) ME (LEFT OF NIKI, CAMERA ON THE READY), FILMING THE DOCUMENTARY FEATURETTE FOR LE MANS, STEVE MCQUEEN'S RACING MOVIE.
A CREW OF 26 PEOPLE IS MANNING THE 70 MM CAMERA IN THE FOREGROUND AND THEY ARE ABOUT TO FILM THE CROWD BEHIND US.
I AM SHOOTING WITH A HAND-HELD 16 MM CAMERA. NIKI AND I ARE SHOOTING LOW BUDGET DOCUMENTARY STYLE, AS A TWO MAN TEAM, AND WE ARE ABOUT TURN 180 DEGREES AND FILM THE SAME CROWD.
NIKI IS DIRECTOR AND ART DIRECTOR, AND I AM THE WRITER, PRODUCER, EDITOR, CAMERAMAN, AND EVERTHING ELSE.

You just want to tell the visual story you've come up with. So you well may ask, *Why do I have to become involved with all the details of who does what?* If your intention is to be a one man band, you don't have to. But don't underestimate the process. Your days of low budget filmmaking will involve an intense combination of physical exertion and mental stress.

There are moments when do-It-yourself vidmaking can be like singing and dancing and running a marathon all at the same time while the road shifts beneath your feet. Not that you can't do it—but don't make light of what it takes to be a solo or semi-solo filmmaker. Having made up your mind for any number of reasons that you will be the driving creative force behind your project, what team members will you persuade to help you realize your vision?

At some point down the glorious trail of your career you may have the resources and the need to add other crew members. At that point, it will help to mull the job descriptions of the various crew members on an average shoot, that is to think of them by their function, by what they add to your storytelling. Production crews are divided by people who pay the salaries into above-the-line and below-the-line categories. The distinction between *above* and *below* is somewhat like the division in military services between officers and troopers. The officers give the orders and the troopers carry them out. Actually, it's good to think about these things *now.* You see, for every person you don't hire, you or some member of your tiny, overworked band will have to pick up the slack.

In bigger budget vids and films, above-the-line
includes the producer(s), the director, the writer(s) (who may or
may not be invited to the set) and the actors. It may also (but
often does not) include the director of photography. Interesting,
but what do these people actually do?

<u>SOMEHOW YOU WILL FIND WAYS</u>TO DO EVERYTHING RIGHT AS POSSIBLE.

**MINIMALIST LOW BUDGET ABOVE-THE-LINE
SITUATION**

Executive Producer – *You, a friend, or wealthy Aunt Aggie*
Producer – *You.*
Writer – *More than likely, you again.*
Director – *The very busy and quickly overburdened you.*

Having written your own script, you will be able to go about realizing your vision. By following the steps outlined in this how to guide, you will be able to make vids of high quality.

As a low budget filmmaker, you can avoid many problems that come with bigger budgets and more complex vids and films. But if you are any good—and of course you are, or you wouldn't have found yourself attracted to this book—you will progress, and as your productions become more complex, your cast and crew will multiply accordingly, as will your production headaches. You will probably, at some point, want to hire a Unit Production Manager to handle details, but if you hire a director, you give away creative control, as well as many other elements of control over the finished product. In fact, once you hire a director, if he feels you are being troublesome, he can bar you from the set. (Yes, you're paying him, and you can fire him, but what a mess!)

When you hire a director, you give away almost all creative control over the project you, yourself, wrote and developed. In the case of small budget films, you as the producer can be the writer and the director, keeping all the creative juices under your own hat. If you do this, you will save money, but I believe in low budget vids it is the best way to go.

Your Assignment

Visualize yourself on the set: Are you going to be a one-man band? If you are shooting a documentary, or even filming 'reality' style, this will be easier than if you intend dramatic or choreographed action scenes.

Assuming there will be some dramatic scenes, which members of the crew will you absolutely need? In shooting extreme low budget, the answer to this probe is that you yourself the jack-of-all-trades, will be the only above-the-line person on the set.

14 - BELOW THE LINE

"Makeup! Makeup? Where the f*ing hell is makeup?"**
--Assistant Director yelling on the set of a Disney movie. Twenty five people are standing around because Genevieve Bujold has shine on her forehead.

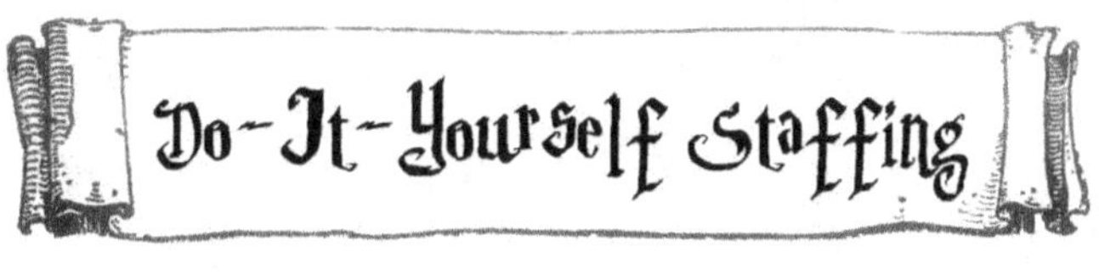

YOUR MINIMALIST LOW BUDGET BELOW-THE-LINE

Camera – *One to three people, or maybe you.*
Sound – *One or two people. Maybe you.*
Lighting – *One to three people. Maybe you. Maybe nobody.*
Misc – *Two or three positive people who solve problems as they present themselves.*

Low budget filmmaking is about calculated risks, analyzing people, hiring the right ones, and trusting them to do a good job. Or taking the time and energy to do it right, yourself. Let your budget be the deciding factor; the rule of thumb is, hire as many good people as you can afford and do the rest yourself.

ART DIRECTOR BRONCO BRADLEY MERVILLE'S VERSATILITY AND POSITIVE ATTITUDE WAS VERY HELPFUL ON THE "EXTINCTION" SHOOT. HE FUNCTIONED NOT ONLY AS LOCATION ART DIRECTOR, HE ALSO WORKED ON SPECIAL EFFECTS AND TOOK STILL PHOTOGRAPHY SHOTS TO RECORD SETUPS AND THE CAST AND CREW IN ACTION. UNIONS TEND TO RESTRICT WHO CAN DO WHAT, BUT ON LOW BUDGET FILMS YOU NEED PROBLEM SOLVERS, AND PEOPLE OF GOOD WILL AND IMAGINATION WHO CAN PITCH IN AND GET THE JOB DONE, NO MATTER WHAT.

An ideal size for a moderately low budget short film is a quartet or at the most, six or seven people if you need a sound crew. The functions are simple to describe: camera, lighting, sound, makeup and wardrobe, and a general category of everything else, including props, driver and running out for sandwiches.

The below-the-line functions you absolutely can not do without are camera, lighting and sound. Today's modern video cameras include sound, so if you are shooting video, you may not need a sound engineer and a boom mike man. But if you choose to go this way, remember you will be tied to the ambient noise in the area. That means when a truck or an airplane goes by or somebody coughs or sneezes, you may need to do a second or third or 20th take to make sure the sound is acceptable.

If you are your own cinematographer, you can get a good sense of whether or not the scene was framed right. However, this takes your attention away from the actor's performance, so use your playback mode to study the take before approving it and going on to the next shot.

As a vidmaker, you cannot escape conflicting ideas of how a film is going to turn out, no matter what your budget may be. The actors, the crew and even curious passersby will have opinions, as is human nature. Still, as a do-it-yourself vidmaker, you will find yourself with creative freedom and opportunities that not even Hollywood directors enjoy. It is your film in every way imaginable. You are the boss, and that is a wonderful and rare feeling for a creative person.

WHEN WORKING FOR A MAJOR STUDIO, THE WATERS PART BEFORE YOU. UNION AND CITY OFFICIALS ARE VERY HELPFUL, AND FLOWERS AND BAGELS AND CREAMED CHEESE SHOWS UP MYSTERIOUSLY ON THE SET. BUT WHEN YOU ARE A LOW BUDGET INDY PRODUCER, ALL THAT GOOD WILL CAN DISAPPEAR LIKE MORNING MIST LEAVING THAT LITTLE LAKE IN CENTRAL PARK. *SO THE WORD TO THE LOW BUDGET VIDMAKER IS TO TRUST NO ONE. BE AS CLEVER AS A FOX, AS WARY AS A LEAN AND HUNGRY COYOTE. GET WHAT YOU WANT, GET IT RIGHT, GET IT FAST, AND GET ON TO THE NEXT SHOT.*

Lighting can be tricky and is a special problem for low budget vidmaking. When moving from shot to shot, continuity starts to plague the one man band. You have to keep the ball rolling, and yet you have to keep track of everything. Where was the light coming from in the last shot? No, that actor can't suddenly be chewing gum. Is the actress actually wearing *a different blouse? Yes, of course the other one had blood stains, and goddamn it that last shot has to match this shot!* It is a good idea to commission your most trusted assistant to keep track of continuity on his or her copy of your shooting script.

Pay special attention to food shoots. It can take a small army of specialists to make ordinary food look right. Of course, in the scene shown above with the dog and the cat the action that's about to take place is more important than how the food looks. But such is not always the case. I did a commercial for Toshiba microwave ovens that featured a pan shot over a table filled with the many types of food one could cook with that oven—roasts, turkeys, casseroles, pies and cakes—and so on. We needed multiple specialized food production experts, three of every example of food, and lighting was a nightmare.

JUST A FEW OF THE THREE DOZEN PEOPLE IT TAKES TO DO A FOOD SHOOT: ON THE SET OF A COMMERCIAL FOR TOSHIBA MICROWAVE OVENS. (L TO R: AGENCY ART DIRECTOR, PRODUCER/DIRECTOR *ME*, ACCOUNT EXECUTIVE HUNTER FINCH, FREE LANCE FOOD PREP LADY.

Lighting cars can also be a horror. I once gave a lighting director an hour to light a new silvery colored Ford and he huffed off the set, never to return. I got his assistant to do it, and it looked *awful,* like a car made of greasy grey mud. On the other hand, action sequences and high speed chases are different, and a streaky, grainy look can add to the dramatic impact of the shot.

Courtesy Michael Keyser, Autosports Marketing Associates, Ltd.

When filming low budget, it helps to start by visualizing your production with the most necessary crew and then weed out people as you think things through. It's your idea, and you have adapted it to a script, so you don't have to hire a writer. If you are going to personally direct (and you should), that problem is also solved. Then, if you also declare yourself the producer, you can start working on auditioning actors and actresses and weeding out the below-the-line people you don't think you need. Remember, every person you decide not to add to your crew adds to the time and energy you personally must expend to get the best possible results.

Walk yourself through every shot on your storyboard, determining just how you intend to capture each moment of your story.

Imagine yourself without lighting. Without at least one production assistant. Without sound people. Without a camera operator.

Without lighting, you have to shoot daylight and outdoors...or be satisfied with a murky and inconsistent look throughout. With an understaffed crew, you'll be waiting for lighting.

Without a sound mixer and boom person you may get by with in-camera sound. But be doubly careful because ambient BG sound will be forever linked to dialogue.

Without a cameraman, you will be distracted from directing talent to the point of insanity.

15 - SCHEDULE IT

"In filmmaking, it's the little things that you take for granted that always kill you. Everything seems like a little pebble from a distance and then you get closer and it turns out to be a boulder."

--Jan Williams, Disney producer of "Condorman" and "The Last Flight of Noah's Ark"

You may say *bad things will never happen to me.* Truth is, they happen to all low budget vidmakers. Stars argue over motivation and interpretation, get hangovers or go missing. Cameramen break a lens, catch the flu or a train to Memphis. Lighting men fall off buildings, get married or join the foreign legion. All you can do is you best, and as your shoot days loom closer you should provide a tight schedule for your shoot. Lock down the Who, What, When, Where and How. Make sure everybody gets a copy of your daily schedule, whether by twitter, email, fax or pony express.

REMEMBER YOUR FOUR "W's" AND ONE "H". FORGETTING ANYTHING IMPORTANT ON A SHOOT DAY WILL DESTROY YOU:

The Who includes all cast and crew who have to be on the set.
The What includes scripts and the lighting and camera equipment, props, effects, food, and restroom facilities.
The When is the exact time each person must show up on the set. If lighting needs an hour to set up, you schedule them to arrive before cast members.
The Where is the location. Be sure to include travel time in your calculations.
The How involves all the abstract calculations that somebody is sure to forget. For instance: *Wear boots because it's going to be muddy. Eat breakfast before you get to the location. Check your gas as there are no Chevron stations in this desert.*

Once everybody agrees on the schedule, you have to be sure everybody who needs to be anywhere knows it. Some producers use email, fax, texting or phone calls. Some use all four methods. If sky writing helps, I recommend it. Here's the sort of communication about detail that is essential for your shoot to run smoothly:

Dear All,
We look forward to all of your hard efforts on the upcoming shoot scheduled for Tues, June 20th. You will all have reservations at the Motel 6 in Mojave for the night before on June 19th. Give or take by traffic, it's about a 2 hour drive from LA to Mojave. From LA you'd take the 405 N to the 5N and then stay right to get on the 14 Highway.
Here's the Motel 6 info:
16958 Hwy 58
Mojave, CA 93501
Tel # 661-824-4571
It's at the juncture of Hwy 58 & 14. Look for big orange Motel 6 sign – they'll keep the light on for you.
We will be filming at 2 sites:
1. **Rogers Rd. & Neualia (near the city, Cantil)** This location is off Highway 14 and is approximately 15 miles north of Mojave.
 Call time is 5:30am for Crew except Heidi Catlin (talent) & Ashlea Perry (Make-up artist).
 Directions to site:
--From Mojave, take Hwy 14 North
--Approximately 15 miles north of Mojave, take a Right on Rogers Rd. It's a side road that maybe hard to see from the Highway. **(See attached picture & map of it so you can see the road from the highway to get a better sense – in the picture, you'll see a Stop Sign from Rogers Rd to Hwy 14) You'll know that you missed Rogers Rd if you keep heading north on Hwy 14 and get to Jawbone Station.**
--Go to the end of Rogers Rd and take a Left at the intersect. on to Neualia (1   road available off Rogers)
--Less than 10 yards is the first location to park right off the highway.
After the shots of the biker on the road & the tortoise close ups scuddling off the road, we'll be heading immediately to the Red Rock Cliffs.
2. **Red Rock Cliffs (Red Rock Canyon)** approximately 7 miles N of Rogers Road from the 1st location.
Call time for Heidi & Ashlea is 7:30am- to meet up w/ rest of Crew after 1st location is finished.
Directions to site:
--Head back to Rogers Rd and make a Right on the Hwy 14 (north)
--You'll see signs of the upcoming Red Rock Canyons and notice that the rock formation change.
--Make a right at the sign stating "Red Rock Canyons, Ricardo Campgrounds" **The sign says to make a left but you'll be making a right at this sign on to a dirt road to head into the Red Cliffs area for our shoot.** Park cars near the outhouse area.
--Attached is a picture of the turn-off w/ the sign. There really isn't a good map on mapquest showing the turn-off. Of course, we'll caravan in the morning from Mojave to not miss the turn-offs from the highway.
We'll be in contact w/ you all this week. The production hotline is my cell # 310-840-5200.
Thank you,
Matt Klawitter

<u>LEAVING NOTHING TO CHANCE</u> FOR THE EXTINCTION SHOOT, OUR PRODUCER MATT KLAWITTER EMAILS INSTRUCTIONS AND THEN FOLLOWS UP WITH PHONE CALLS.

Simple enough, right? Well, okay, below is a storyboard for a 30 second commercial.   With what you've learned in earlier chapters, how many days would it take to film? You think two days…three at the most? Well, you're almost right. We did get the party and the beauty shots in one day in Malibu. But there were no waves on the West Coast, and because we had to meet air dates for our television buy, we had to fly to Hawaii. Had to, you see.

Courtesy Kelly/Nason Advertising Los Angeles & United Vintners.

Using the best information you have available in the days before you shoot, plan the details so everything runs as smoothly as possible. You provide a tight schedule to have the best possible chance to get it done. There will be mistakes and setbacks, but knowing your schedule gives you the best chance to shift the shooting order and to pick up the slack. Stay confident and in control, *because your show must go on.*

Build a list of the cast and crew members who
will be on your shoot. Be sure you have their
phone numbers and e-mail addys.

Type out a call sheet clearly detailing the who,
what, when, where and how of your shoot.
Make certain you have attended for their
creature comforts. If you are an exceptionally
paranoid producer (as I am), you will do a
sheet for each day.

16 - SHOOT IT

"As a director on the set you live in two worlds; you have to see and feel and hear and experience everything and yet you have to separate yourself to see and feel and hear and experience how this special piece of the puzzle that you are filming at that very moment will fit seamlessly into the whole of the finished film."

--John Sturges, famous film director, to Nikita Knatz, after a long day on the set at Le Mans.

We talk about "shoot days" as if production is set in stone. Of course, when you shoot your own vid, nothing is set in rock. A shoot day may be a half hour when you can get the shot you need or ten days of half hours. But, working from your storyboard and knowing what is possible, you can figure out how best to capture your vision. There is an undeniable advantage to shooting in sequence, or in batches of shots. But when this isn't possible, you gather your resources and shoot when you can. It doesn't matter if you shoot one or three days, or if you shoot an hour or two every day for a month. Just don't give up on your vision or your dream of seeing your vid through to completion.

Our crew on "Extinction" turned out to be a producer, director/writer (me), assistant director, cameraman, assistant cameraman, sound man, boom man, makeup/hairdresser (tripled by handling wardrobe), art director (who also helped with continuity, special effects and photographic stills), turtle wrangler, go-pher, and a few helpful hangers-on. That may seem like a lot of people for a simple video with one actress and a desert tortoise, two characters who do little more than talk to each other and walk around in the middle of nowhere. Oh, and lest I forget, there was also a bit-part bike rider and a coyote in

the script, and they both had to be dealt with.   The way it turned
out, situations and difficulties came up as they always do.
Emergencies had to be dealt with. And the various members of
the crew, both above and below-the-line, found themselves
scrambling for solutions to usual and unusual production
problems.

**Tuesday, June 20, 2006. The day dawns bright and
clear for our "Extinction"** shoot on the Mojave Desert.
Everybody shows up on time and the weather looks like it is
going to behave. (Even though we have missed April by six
weeks.) We begin with a few establish shots of the rugged and
dry wastelands. Then we get into the biker sequence. The biker
roars past the Tortoise, throwing an empty beer can at him as
he goes. We have trouble when I realize I need an *assistant*
assistant director. I have my AD, but there is nobody a half mile
down the road with the biker who can talk to my AD who must
alert them when the turtle was ready. Problem solved by Sister
Mary Immaculata, one of the eager volunteers who has showed
up to see what they could see.

We move on to the 'littered roadside' shots. It is a seemingly simple enough sequence where Harley-the-tortoise makes his way through roadside trash. I thought we had plenty of garbage, but seeing it for the first time through the lens I was thinking we could have used more, even though passersby were giving us the evil eye for *crapping up the desert.* (We picked it all up after). And Harley's movement, when he moved at all, was, well, slower than a snail's. Was I ever happy we'd hired a *tortoise wrangler* and rented those extra turts! Actually, we'd had no choice, we had to rent a trio of turtles and the wrangler came with them. Desert tortoises are an endangered species, and their work rules would make members of any union green with envy.

WAITING FOR THE TORTOISE. DP PIERS BATH PATIENTLY SITS BEHIND THE SHOT HE LINED UP A HALF HOUR BEFORE WHILE KELLY CANTLY, MY ASSISTANT DIRECTOR, STUDIES HER NOTES AND JAY THE BOOM MIKE MAN LOOKS ON. MY DECISION TO SHOOT UNDER THE AUSPICES OF THE DIRECTOR'S GUILD OF AMERICA MEANT I HAD TO HIRE KELLY. IT WAS A SMART MOVE; ASSISTANT DIRECTORS ARE EXTREMELY HELPFUL FOR ALL BUT THE MOST SIMPLE PRODUCTIONS, AND ONE GOOD ONE IS WORTH AT LEAST A DOZEN PRODUCTION APPRENTICES.

There is a reason for every person on the set. When you set up your own shoots, as you start doubling up on the jobs you personally are performing, you come to appreciate what all those other people do. When we set out to film my dramatic short film "Extinction", the number of below the line people began to mushroom in a way that seriously worried me. As a guild director I knew I would have to hire an assistant. Actually, I came to wish I'd hired two or three.

But, you see, I hadn't budgeted for the *turtle wrangler*. I didn't realize we needed one until two days before the actual shoot. I thought it was a union thing and, being on the desert with nobody around, I could simply ignore the rules. But my producer found out that no animal rental shop in town would rent us some desert tortoises unless they came with an expensive human handler who understood their needs and dispositions.

THERE IS NO BUZZ IN THE WORLD QUITE LIKE DIRECTING. FORTY THINGS ARE FLASHING THROUGH YOUR MIND, FORTY MORE THINGS CALL FOR YOUR ATTENTION, AND YOU ARE TRYING TO STAY IN THE CALM PLACE AT THE CENTER OF YOUR AWARENESS WHERE YOU KNOW YOU HAVE TO KEEP THE FLOW, KEEP THE PACE, KEEP TOTAL CONTROL OVER THE CREATION OF A WORLD THAT ONLY YOU CAN VISUALIZE COMPLETELY— ALL THE TIME MAINTAINING THIS INCREDIBLE BALANCE AND AWARENESS AS THE WORLD OF YOUR STORY SHAPES ITSELF BEFORE YOUR EYES. IN THE PICTURE ABOVE, WHILE I SEEM TO GAZE WITH SERENITY AT THE DISTANT BEAUTY OF THE FAR MOUNTAINS, INSIDE I'M FUMING, FUSSING AND CUSSING *"WHERE IS THAT DAMN TURTLE?!"*

On the set, camera ready, cast in position--this is the point at which you come alive as the director of your story. A director is a writer who paints with visuals, motion and spoken dialogue, fleshing the realities that writers create with their words.

You must accomplish the mundane tasks of setting lights and pushing buttons if you have not hired or persuaded others to perform them for you, for they are a vital necessity to the process. But, beyond that which must be done, you are the sole creator of your universe. As such, you must assure that you shoot adequate footage to clearly carry your story--establish (master) shots, medium & close shots, dialogue sequences, action shots, mood and scenics, and so on...

Be aware of continuity. Beware jarring shifts in attitude and characterization. Shepherd and bully and protect your actors from themselves and each other. Remember: Story Uber Allis. And, when all is shot and in the can, it is YOUR story.

17 - FIRST CUT EDIT

"I think we can fix it in post."
--Anonymous, often heard on the set.

Today's home computer editing systems are so quick and reliable they have driven some of the entrenched Hollywood post-productions entirely out of business. So when you sit down to your computer, input your footage and begin to lay it out on your editing system, you know you will be able to create a workable first cut of your story.

<u>COMPUTER SOFTWARE IS CONSTANTLY BEING UPGRADED, SO I'M NOT</u> SAYING YOU SHOULD RUN OUT AND BUY THIS OR THAT PRODUCT. I PERSONALLY USE CYBERLINK POWERDIRECTOR 9. IT COST ME UNDER A HUNDRED DOLLARS AND I LIKE IT FINE.

Some vidmakers carefully annotate every take. Others just keep a mental log, particularly for short vids. You have to do what is best for you. One good way is to use the same numbering system as your storyboard, which you should be referring to as you edit.

There are alternate theories of how to cut your story. Some vidmakers like to go by feelings. While they will refer to the storyboard to make sure they don't forget any shots or lines of dialogue, they will try to capture the original mood of their idea, why they decided to produce this vid in the first place. Others will stick to the storyboard entirely, realizing they can easily change it at any time. Still others will cut to the action and the sound sense, letting the pacing of the dialogue and the action play in a way that seems most natural.

No one editing style is right for every vid. After all, if you are primarily interested in a tone poem of nature shots, you could do well to cut to appropriate classical music. But if you are recording a skateboarding adventure, hip-hop music might be a better idea. Sometimes vids are cut to the actual lyrics in a song (but if this is the case, you would have started way back when you wrote your script, or at this point you'll see you probably don't have the right footage). Most often, though, *the story is the thing*, and you will want to find the pacing that is most satisfactory to your original idea.

IF YOU OR YOUR FRIENDS HAVE BEEN PERFECTING YOUR GARAGE BAND FOR YEARS, HERE'S YOUR CHANCE TO WRITE AN ORIGINAL SONG AND TURN IT INTO A ONE-OF-A-KIND VIDEO.

Assuming you are basically happy that your rough cut is solid, that is, that it tells your story the way you intended it, you are at the point where you can move on to finish your film. You might want to refine the cuts, to make the timing of certain scenes more to your liking, but then you are ready to use your editing software to place transition effects, fades and various wipes to get from one scene to the next. You'll probably find that your editing software will provide you with (too many) choices.

Using your home computer and your home editing
system, assemble your rough video, using your
storyboard as a prime reference and guide.

As you assemble, note down all potential problems.
Realize that this is a rough cut. Sleep on it.
Show it to friends, loved ones and antagonists.
Mull, ponder and question everything you've done.

Decide if you need to shoot additional footage or not.

18 - SOUND

You have choices here. Hopefully you thought most of them out when you were scripting and drawing up your storyboard. Still, if you didn't, it's not the end of the world. If you are building your vid from stills or are shooting nature footage, there is little reason for lip sync sound.

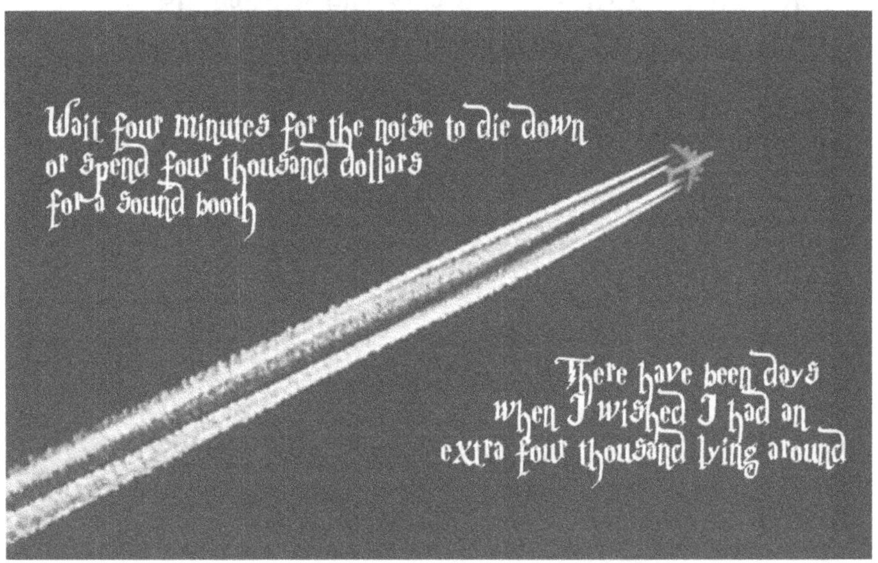

If you recorded sound when you shot, you probably have already laid that down in your first cut. If it is muddy or full of annoying background noises like cars or airplanes, you can use software to 'scrub' it, that is, clean it up somewhat, and maybe add some timbre or presence to the voices. If the dialogue is too bad, you can re-record it, though this is a difficult process requiring skill on the part of the actor(s) reading the lines.

You may intend to do your own Voice Over Narration. This is a great way to personalize your vid, and it's not nearly as difficult as it may seem. A home recording rig is inexpensive and easy to use. Some computers come ready to go with a jack to input sounds from a microphone. If you do record VO Narration, it will end up on a track separate from the sound you recorded when you originally shot your video, giving you the ability to increase or decrease the volume and to slop it around in your edit, moving it forward and back until you find the exactly right spot.

I HAVE NARRATED NOVELS AND BOOKS AND DOZENS OF COMMERCIALS AND TRAILERS FROM THIS SIMPLE, LOW COST RIG THAT I SET UP AND CONNECTED TO MY COMPUTER. DON'T TELL ME YOU CAN'T DO THE SAME—OR EVEN BETTER. NOTE: THAT ROUND WAFFLE THING IN FRONT OF THE MIKE KEEPS ME FROM POPPING MY 'P' SOUNDS. IT COST ME 15 BUCKS USED ON EBAY.

Some vidmakers swear they will never record their own voice, not even in the privacy of their own bedroom with the blankets pulled over their heads. Fair enough. But most people like you have at least a dozen best friends, pals or buddies who would be glad to belt out a song or two at a karaoke bar. And with a little direction from you, those best buds will give you the perfect narration for your vid. After all (you'll tell them), it could be the start of a great career in radio, or voice announcing on television commercials. You can't begin to start in that business without a demo reel, and you'll be providing quality no-cost samples for them.

VOICE OVER NARRATION – THINGS TO REMEMBER

When you do your own narration:

Take yourself seriously but without pomposity.

Figure who you are and be that person until the record light goes off.

Voice people are hired for how they sound, not what they know.

You never know who you can become until you put on that headset.

Never pop your "p's" But if you do, it can be fixed.

Cup your ear like Gary Owens if you think it will help. Gary said he never knew exactly why he did it, either.

When recording professional voice talent:

Voices are uniquely characteristic to the individual talent.

Generally speaking, the more famous, the narrower the range.

Don't ask Sponge Bob Squarepants to do Darth Vadar, but…

You can ask Bob to do Bob impersonating Darth.

Pacing is as important as breathing.

If you need another take.blame the soundman. They are used to it.

*If you **are** the soundman, blame equipment failure.*

When recording amateur voice talent:

Goof around a lot to get their mind off it.

Tell them it is a practice take, but hit the record button.

Blame overhead airplanes or mating ferrets if you need another take.

Cut the whole thing together after they leave.

Have three or four back-up voices in mind.

Voice Over Narration shouldn't be anything extraordinary in this age of relatively powerful home computers. You don't even need to build a little sound booth in your garage or cabana. Most computers come with the ability to record sound, and one major secret to recording decent narration tracks is to buy a good mike. And with add on software programs (I use an inexpensive program called **SoundSoap** 2) you can scrub much if not all of the air conditioning hiss and refrigerator hum from your sound track.

THIS IS A PICTURE FRAME INTENDED TO CONVEY COPY POINTS WITHOUT A VOICE OVER NARRATOR. SUCH TECHNIQUES ARE OFTEN USED IN BOOK TRAILERS BY AUTHORS WHO HAVE LITTLE BUDGET TO ADVERTISE THEIR BOOKS. WHEN TELLING A DRAMATIC STORY, "ART CARD" FRAMES SLOW DOWN THE PACE OF THE VIDEO, NOT ALWAYS A GOOD THING. .

If recording even the simplest narration is outside your comfort zone, you can make a good video the old fashioned silent movie way, using art cards or superimposing text to carry the story. On the other hand, you can set yourself up to record clean professional narration, and record the tracks yourself, for very little money, probably less than your monthly tab at Starbucks for those *grande lattes* and blueberry scones you love so dearly…oh, wait, that's me I'm talking about.

Many super-low budget vidmakers create stories that do not need voice over narration, particularly when making the popular book trailers you see on the internet. You can tell a story that way, but it does handicap the easy flow of the tale telling. In shop talk, the pacing of your visuals is limited to the time viewers need to read the art cards. The secret to success then becomes keeping the art cards short and pithy so your entire presentation moves along.

Music is always a nice idea, and you will want to edit this in on its own separate music track. If you have access to a local band, or play an instrument yourself, that free music track can establish a mood or heighten key moments in the video. And your *real true* friends will not hesitate to give you the use rights for no money at all. When you become a big deal vidmaker, you will, of course, pay them plenty, and in the mean time, there's always the free publicity. But if they prove not your *absolute real true* friends, or if you don't know a garage band, stock music is available from the internet at very reasonable prices, and there are other places where innovative DJ's and amateur musicians will be delighted to let you use their music for a credit on the end of your vid.

Don't forget special sound effects. If you've got chickens, a tire blow out at high speed or guns going off, you will want to build a special Sound EFX track. Don't forget outdoor noises like the wind or chirping birds where those effects would be expected, otherwise your track may sound strange, somehow not right for the great outdoors or an echo-filled cavern. You'll find most sound effects are very specific to the visuals…and you can always use tricks like coconut shells on a wooden table for clupping horse hooves or shaking aluminum foil for storm noises. If you can't figure out how to make do-it-yourself sound effects, lucky for you there are a wide variety of cheap stock sounds available on the internet.

When you get your various sound tracks laid down and cut in the right spots against the visuals, your editing software will give you the ability to set the proper sound levels, and after some trial and error while you do a few test runs to get things right, you can mix the sounds to give you your mixed sound track. Not that you can't change it later on, but it's good at this point to hear a sound mix against the rough cut picture.

Build your sound effects and your music tracks.

If you want a voice over narration, now is the time
to record it and to build that track.

Clean each individual sound track, if needed,
including your original dialogue tracks.

Mix your sound elements--Music, Sound efx
Dialogue, and VO Narration if you have that.

Study your vid from the point of view of
a total stranger, or even an alien from another
solar system. Are you telling your story clearly?
If doubts linger, consider using a few lines of
storytelling narration superimposed over your
visuals, perhaps at the opening, or at key points.

19 - VISUAL TRICKERY

"If you don't have a story, you're hopeless. But if you do, the slick look of your show—whether shot on 16 mm, 35 or video—most certainly helps with the telling of it."

--Harold Orton, British producer famous for his tenacity, good humor, and penny-pinching ways.

The transitions from scene to scene are more important than they may seem at first glance. Viewers see them as simply a series of cuts or fades and pay them little attention, if any at all—and this is as it should be. Any transition that is obvious isn't working and should be reconsidered.

Think mood and style when selecting the transitions for your film. If you are building a quiet dream sequence, you won't want jarring or explosive transition moves (except for that moment when the monster shows up, if there is a monster.) Long dissolves might work best here. With film in the old days, transitions could be uncertain, depending on the chemical nature of the film and the way the two pieces interacted across the dissolve. But with vid, you have far more control, and can quickly adjust the length of any dissolve.

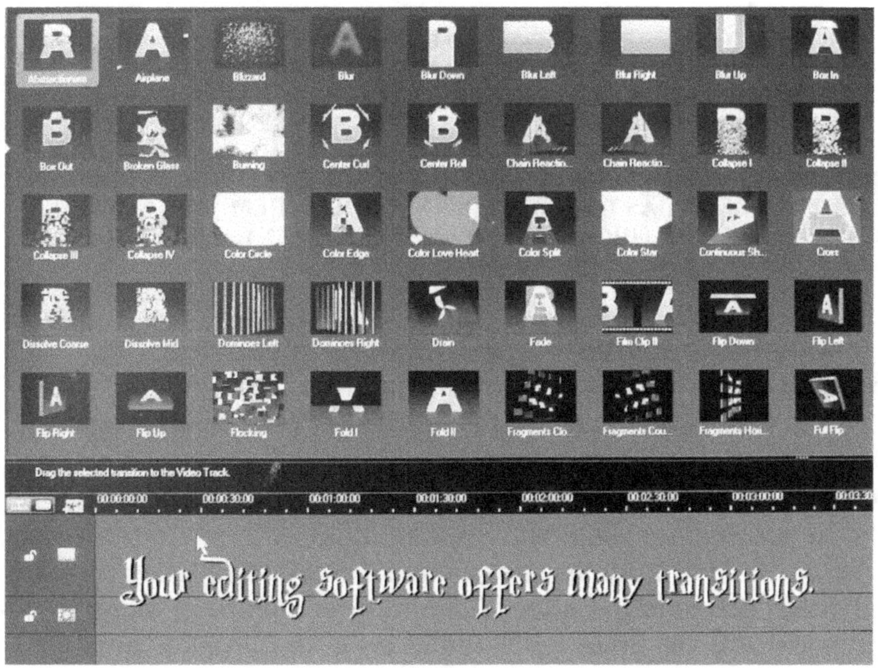

Your problem could well be that your video editing software offers you *scores of different transitions*. Choose carefully, as you don't want them to overpower or interfere with your story. And it is not as simple as just selecting between cuts or fades. The length of the dissolve is important; a dissolve might take several seconds, indicating a dream-like state or languid tranquility. On the other hand, a very disturbing effect can be obtained by interjecting flash cuts of only a few frames of violence or horror into an otherwise peaceful scene.

<u>SPECIAL EFFECTS USED TO BELONG</u> TO BIG BUDGET STORIES—BUT NO MORE. YOUR VID CAN DELIGHT AND AMAZE AS FAR AS YOUR IMAGINATION WILL TAKE IT. STREAK FOOTAGE LIKE THIS IS EASY TO CREATE WITH ANY DECENT VID CAMERA. YOU'VE SEEN IT MANY TIMES, MAYBE IN SHOTS OF NIGHTTIME CARS PASSING ON THE FREEWAY OR THOSE OPEN LENS SHOTS WHERE THE STARS ARE CAPTURED IN CIRCLES OF LIGHT IN THE SKY AS THE EARTH SPINS UNDER THEM. BUT NEVER FORGET, THIS IS JUST TRICKERY AND EMBELLISHMENT. THE REAL MAGIC IS IN YOUR STORY AND THE TELLING OF IT.

Beyond transitions, you might be pleasantly surprised at the degree of control you have over your video footage in post production. While you can't rewrite your story or make your actors give a more convincing performance, you can groom, twitch and enrich the footage you have in a variety of ways. If you use a stills shot, you can make moves on the scene, panning or zooming as you wish, within the limits of the numbers of pixels in the shot. Assuming you were in focus to begin with, you still have a latitude to be able to make these moves. You can make a quiet sunset out of one stills shot, gradually dissolving down to the same shot with less light intensity until the entire screen goes dark. You can cause a scene to go blood red, to go from black-and-white to color, or from color to sepia (indicating a move back in time to a long-gone generation). In fact, you can achieve a professional look and feel that is far superior to the best 16 mm film projects of a few decades ago.

THIS IS THE SAME SHOT IN ALL FOUR FRAMES: I PULLED OFF TO THE SIDE OF THE ROAD AND SNAPPED THIS BLEAK DESERT STILL SHOT. LATER IN POST, I GRADUALLY DARKENED THE SHOT AND CAUSED IT TO GO MORE AND MORE RED UNTIL THERE WAS JUST A BAND OF JAGGED, BLOOD RIMMED CLOUDS ACROSS THE SKY. A PERFECT ENDING PIECE OF FOOTAGE OVER WHICH I WAS ABLE TO RUN END CREDITS.

You can shape and even *fix* some unsatisfactory elements of your film after the completion of principal photography. With today's low cost, high quality cameras and home editing systems—and your own creativity— you can produce do-it-yourself videos with a remarkable degree of quality. There is such a wide variety of low cost visual and sound special effects available from stock libraries that you will have to employ restraint to stay under budget and keep your project on target.

DON'T FORGET STOCK FOOTAGE. WHETHER YOU ARE WORKING WITH STILLS, LIVE ACTION, OR A COMBO OF THE TWO, STOCK FOOTAGE CAN SAVE YOUR BACON AT A VERY LOW COST. BUT DON'T DEPEND ON IT. THAT SHOT YOU NEED MOST MAY NOT BE AVAILABLE *WHEN YOU ABSOLUTELY HAVE TO HAVE IT.*

SOME THINGS YOU CAN SOMETIMES FIX IN POST

Mismatches in *color,.brightness and lighting.*
Poor quality in *dialogue and background sounds.*
Confusing story continuity *can sometimes be corrected by adding voice over audio narration or supers identifying time, date and/or place.*
Lack of coverage *can be corrected to some extent through use of slow motion, stutter cuts or other filmic trickery.*

THINGS YOU WILL HAVE TROUBLE FIXING IN POST

Confused or vague initial concept. *The most unforgivable, unfixable sin.*

Poor writing. *Bad dialogue, holes in the storytelling*

Bad acting. *If it's not working out on the set, let them go At once and find somebody else. Better lose a few hours or a day than end up with a vid that doesn't work.*

Inferior direction. *Inadequate coverage, unsteady acting performances, lack of cohesive style*

Incompetent camera work. *There's no way to fix soft focus after footage is in the can.*

WHEN YOUR STORY CALLS FOR AN EXCITED EMOTIONAL STATE, THIS BLURRED IMAGERY CAN WORK TO SHOW HASTE AND ANXIETY

BUT WHEN YOUR VISUAL INTENT IS TO PRESENT CALMNESS AND CLARITY, YOU WILL WANT SHARP FOCUS AND CRISP PHOTOGRAPHY.

<u>**THE DISNEY PEOPLE**</u> **CRAFTED, SCULPTED, BUILT A MOLD AND POURED TWO OR THREE OF THESE METAL WONDERS FOR ME. ON SCREEN, THIS THING FALLS OVER WITH A MIGHTY CLANG. BUT TODAY YOU, AS A LOW BUDGET DO-IT-YOURSELF VIDMAKER CAN ELECTRONICALLY CREATE THIS SAME EFFECT…PRACTICALLY FOR FREE!**

<u>**IT TOOK HOURS IN A COSTLY EDIT BAY**</u> **TO CREATE THIS ILLUSION, AND COST THOUSANDS OF DOLLARS. TODAY, YOU CAN CREATE A SIMILAR ILLUSION WITH YOUR COMPUTER AT A FRACTION OF THE COST.**

**You can use your transitions to create effects
beyond their original intent:** In 2010, I needed to produce a
short book trailer for my murder mystery novel FOUL. The story
was about an old NFL scandal that was covered up by some
very skillful killers. I wanted to visually show a transition from
football to murder, but I didn't have the budget to do anything
more than stills photography. One sunny morning I traveled to
my front lawn and snapped a stills shot of some grass (Frame
#1). Then I took a football and filmed that against a clean
background, actually a piece of beige canvas. I knew that,
using Adobe Photoshop, I could make the canvas disappear
and place the football on the grass background. (Frame #2). I
manipulated a rough "Hawiian" football, a joke artifact made out
of a dried and wrinkled coconut shell, into the same size as the
regular football (Frame #3). Then I darkened the 'coconut'
football, giving it a sinister look. (Frame #4) And finally, I used
a stock shot of a whitened human skull and rotated that to the
same angle as the coconut shell football. (Frame #5)
Dissolving from one through five created a very creepy
sequence—something was rotten in an old NFL championship
game and our hero had to figure out what it was.

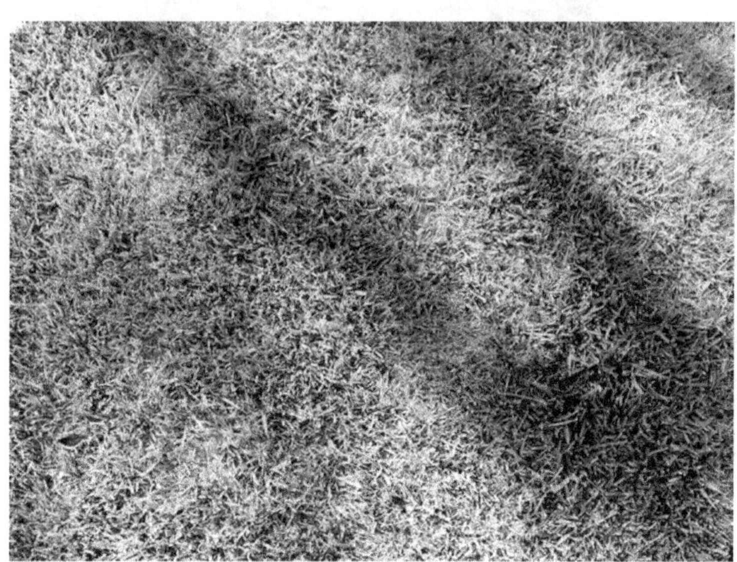

FRAME #1: **GRASS BACKGROUND OF A FOOTBALL FIELD**

**FRAME #2: REGULAR FOOTBALL DISSOLVES ONTO THE GRASS BG.
BECAUSE THE BACKGROUND NEVER CHANGES, THE VIEWER'S ATTENTION
FOCUSES ON THE FOOTBALL,THAT SEEMS TO FADE IN OUT OF THIN AIR.**

**FIGURE #3: WHILE THE GRASS BG REMAINS THE SAME, THE FOOTBALL
DISSOLVES INTO A SHRUNKEN, SOMEWHAT WEIRD FOOTBALL.**

FIGURE #4: THE WEIRD FOOTBALL BECOMES EVEN STRANGER, DARKENING AS IF IT IS WITHERING.

FIGURE #5: THE STRANGE FOOTBALL NOW DISSOLVES INTO A SKULL, COMPLETING THE VISUAL COMMUNICATION THAT A MURDER HAS TAKEN PLACE THAT INVOLVED PROFESSIONAL FOOTBALL.

There is a true revolution going on in the world of visual storytelling, and you can take advantage of it. You already know how to tell a story, and this manual is here to remind you of the simple steps to ensure your success.

MY CURRENT HOME POST SYSTEMS & EQUIPMENT

Presonus Firebox – *Sound Amplifier.   You don't need this, but I wanted it because I record my novels as audio books*

Audio-Technica – *AT3035 mike, with small standup boom and a waffle to prevent 'popping' sounds.*

CuBase – *Recording and sound editing software. I bought the beginner's version and find it more than sufficient for my needs.*

Audacity – *A free program for maneuvering sound from single to mono ear buds and helpful in adjusting sound levels, and so on.*

SoundSoap 2 – *An easy to use software program, helpful for reducing ambient noises like refrigerator hums and cat wails.*

Podiobooks – *A wonderful site that will not only walk you through building your own low cost home sound rig , but will take you step-by-step through podcasting and teach you to record your own books. And, if you follow their instructions carefully enough, they will offer your audio books on their website. www.podiobooks.com*

Stock 20 – *Terrific stock music cues at a low) price.* *www.stock20.com*

iStock Photography – *Great assortment, pay as you go.* *www.istockphoto.com*

As a vidmaker new worlds open up to you—the worlds of your own imagination—and they can carry you as far as your storytelling can fly. In these chapters I have given you the mental process to carry your ideas into actual short videos. The tools—the cameras, editing systems and software—may change, but the process and the problems will always remain the same. If you remember to analyze your videos in terms of time, money and talent, you will move forward with a positive attitude and become the complete and accomplished vidmaker.

Using your editing software, choose from the bewildering array of dissolves and transitions and incorporate them into your vid.

The key discipline is to choose transitionary effects that make sense in terms of your story, not only the mood, but also what you are communicating.

Now gaze upon what you have created with joy and wonder. And begin to think about what film festivals to enter. The process has been long, but believe it, you are a Vidmaker.